The High Diving Board

HOW TO OVERCOME YOUR FEARS
AND LIVE YOUR DREAMS

*Ken,
Thanks for having
the courage to
live your dreams.
Sandy Schussel*

Sandy Schussel

THE HIGH DIVING BOARD:
How to Overcome Your Fears
and Live Your Dreams

by Sandy Schussel

Printed in the United States of America
First Edition, May 2004

ISBN No. 1-59196-621-3
Published by Brass Ring Coaching
Princeton, NJ

DEDICATION

This book is dedicated to my wife, Hannah, who saved my life in the summer of 1992 and then encouraged me to go out and find the life I really wanted.

ACKNOWLEDGEMENTS

To my father, who taught me compassion, but never overcame his fears.

To my mother, brothers, sister, my wife, my daughters and the dear friends who I know are always there for me, even when we've been out of touch.

To my friends, Susan Rudy and Ed Leefeldt, who gave their valuable time to read this book as I was writing it, and gave me the gift of their valuable feedback.

And to my clients, who remind me every day how exhilarating it is to climb the path to my High Diving Board.

CONTENTS

Introduction.
Why Another Self-Help Book?

By 1990, I was a successful lawyer with a practice that many younger lawyers envied, but I had come to hate my career. My unhappiness was endless and squelched the joy from nearly all of what I might otherwise have viewed as accomplishments. Every day I awoke early, worked until late at night, came home and went to sleep, so that I could get up and do it all over again the next day. Except for my brief moments with my daughters, my life was colorless.

Years before, when I first began practicing law, I believed I had started a career that would bring me adventure and joy; a career about which I could be passionate and that would leave me feeling fulfilled. A few years into it, however, I found it to be a career with long, tedious hours, mountains of paperwork, unhappy people everywhere and endless arguing and posturing. But I believed I was trapped—by the need to support the lifestyle I thought a lawyer was supposed to be living, by the belief that I didn't know what else I wanted to do, and by *fear*… of taking a chance on change.

As the excessive '80s ended, I lost my three largest clients in a period of about fourteen months. One of the businesses went into bankruptcy. The owner of a second business suffered a stroke, and his wife sold off the company to a much larger corporation that had its own lawyers. And the large PBA I had represented for ten years elected a new President whose best friend was a labor attorney. I'm convinced that his mind wasn't made up until he saw me driving the Mercedes I had leased after providing the dealership with some creative accounting of my ability to make lease payments. It was easy for the new PBA president to convince his board that somehow *they* had paid for this car by paying me excessive fees. It wasn't true, but what was true didn't really matter.

Two things were clear: we had to cut expenses, and I had to do something that would force me to give up a career I despised. So, we sold our huge old "money pit" of a home in our exclusive neighborhood in northern New Jersey and found a new home in a pleasant town home community near Princeton. We cut our expenses significantly, but added two hours of commuting to my already ridiculously long days.

The added commute was self-sabotage. I knew that moving so far away would compound my suffering. I wanted to make continuing to be a lawyer so miserable that it would force me to find something else. I didn't know any other way to change my life.

But my life was about to change anyway. On the morning of December 31, 1991, I was driving my wife's red Saab along the highway with my two little girls in the back seat. I was headed for work (another real estate closing) and my daughters were on their way to visit their old baby sitter in northern New Jersey; a nice outing for them.

The heater appeared to be blowing cold and I wanted to make my girls warmer. I thought that I might have somehow inadvertently pushed the air conditioning button on, so I took my eyes off the road for *just a second* to look for it, to press it off. *Just for a second.* But when I looked up again, we had drifted to the left shoulder of the highway. As I moved the wheel to the right gently to ease back onto the road, the front left wheel dropped into the grass median, the long, low front end of the Saab caught the shoulder and the *car began flipping over and over and over in the median at sixty miles per hour.*

As we hurtled through space, my daughter Stefanie was screaming, "Daddy what's happening? Daddy what's happening?" But I couldn't answer her.

I watched in terror—arms flailing, everything moving as if in slow motion—as the sun roof tore away, and frozen earth and debris scraped in through the open hatch each time the sky was below us. The windows blew out, and the roof on the front passenger side—above the only empty seat—collapsed, but we were still flying.

Then, there was silence. The car was still. There were no engine sounds and the highway seemed to no longer exist. I turned to see Stefanie, cowered in the corner and whimpering, but alive and whole. I twisted around a little more to see her little sister, Madeline, who was strapped in behind me. But I couldn't see her face because—*it was covered in blood.* The picture of the red stains on her little yellow ski jacket is still vivid in my memory.

We spent New Year's Eve holding each other tightly all night. But that was *just the beginning* of 1992.

Six months before the accident, I had visited my doctor—my friend Jeffrey—to express concern about a little bleeding problem of my own. Jeffrey had recommended that I visit a gastroenterologist for one of those invasive exams that men, in particular, will do anything to avoid. And so, I avoided it. But now, having survived that accident, I finally found the courage to go for that exam. I mean, after all, if I—we—could survive an accident like that, how bad could whatever it was be?

A month after the accident, I learned that I had colon cancer. From that moment on, my life—our lives—began flipping over and over like that red Saab: extensive surgery at Memorial Sloan Kettering Cancer Center …learning that the disease had already begun to spread…a devastating course of chemotherapy… the cold, inhuman radiation therapy room …bouts of abdominal pain so severe that my frightened children found me crawling on my hands and knees, trying in vain to get away from it…hospitalizations for morphine…coming within hours of death…a second extensive surgery at Sloan Kettering—this time to save my life…being *left open*, like raw meat…

Twice, I was blessed to be able to leave Memorial Sloan Kettering Cancer Center to return home. Each time I left a roommate who never made it back to *his* home. By August, my weight had dropped from a healthy 155 pounds to 112 pounds, and the complications that had made the second surgery necessary had left me totally disabled.

I couldn't work, we were bankrupt, and even my most loyal clients could not wait to see if I'd ever be there for them again.

Towards the end of 1992, as I finally began to mend, I was faced with rebuilding the dreaded law practice, or finding out what I really wanted to do with my life.

My struggle over the next few years to create a new life—one filled with adventure, passion and joy—taught me the lessons about fear and how to master it that I have tried to share in this book. Among other things, I learned how easy it is to delude yourself into believing you've climbed all the way to your High Diving Board, when you've really just settled at a lower board somewhere along the path.

Why another self-help book? If I can help even just a few people propel themselves up the path that leads to their high diving board, it will have been worth all of the effort.

> **F**eel the fear and do it anyway.
> ~ Susan Jeffers ~

1. It's Okay To Be Afraid

"Daddy, I'm afraid. I want to go home."

My daughter, Stefanie, was nine years old. We were standing outside a rehearsal room in the basement of a nearby regional theater. Stefanie was there to audition for a children's part she really wanted in a production of "A Christmas Carol." It was her turn to audition next.

Stefanie had rehearsed a monologue and had sung "Somewhere Over The Rainbow" at least twelve hundred times. But now, standing here in the hallway in the basement of the theater, she was paralyzed with fear. Her own arms were wrapped tightly around her and she hunched over as if she was bracing herself against a strong wind. Tears were filling the outside corners of her large golden brown eyes.

"Daddy, please take me home?"

Her voice was barely audible and it was obvious that the only thing that might get her to move would be if I opened the glass door that led to the sidewalk outside and said, "C'mon, let's go home!" For that, she would have bolted. Otherwise, she was frozen in place. I knew I had to say something to calm her fear, to give her courage, but seeing her there, helpless and immobilized, triggered my own fears. If I had responded with the first thoughts that came into my head, it might have sounded something like this:

"Stefanie, I'm afraid, too! I'm afraid that my battle with cancer isn't really over and that I have very little time left with you. I'm

afraid that the disability that I've been suffering since the last operation is permanent; that this is as good as it's going to get for whatever time I have left. I'm afraid that we've used up all our money and all of our credit, and that we may lose our home; that you'll grow up to resent that I brought you to this affluent community to be the poorest kid here. And I'm afraid that the only work I know how to do is the work that I believe contributed to my getting sick in the first place..."

I was pretty sure that saying something along those lines would not be very helpful to my distraught daughter in her current predicament, so I reached down inside and came up with these words instead:

"Stefanie, honey, it's okay to be afraid. Everybody is afraid. But this is your dream, and afraid or not, you just have to do it."

Stefanie looked up at me and nodded slightly, as if to say, "You're right, Daddy, that's just what I needed." She started toward the door of the rehearsal room, tentatively at first and then standing up tall and moving boldly. She auditioned and got the part.

I didn't realize at the time that I had, in that moment, stumbled on what I now know to be a universal truth about fear and courage—and gave my daughter the best advice I may have ever given either of my girls. I also didn't know at the time that it would take me another five years to truly understand and believe those words and to begin to live by them.

I am writing this book in the hope that I can help my readers learn the truth about courage and fear--and how to build one while defying the other—without having to stumble through another five years until it all makes sense.

> **O**f all base passions, fear is the most accursed.
>
> ~ William Shakespeare ~

2. Living Your Dreams

WADDAYAWANT?

No, I mean it. What do you want? What's your dream? Even people who feel successful and those who feel, as I do, that their lives are abundant, have dreams that they are not living—not pursuing. Some of us have hundreds of unfulfilled dreams that we're no closer to achieving than we were yesterday or the day before, last year or ten years ago. What's yours?

Maybe it involves money: more money for more toys; money for creature comforts; money for security or to be able to give more to the causes you care about. Maybe it involves fame or, at least, recognition; or some more control over your life. Maybe your dream is about having a more fulfilling career or more fulfilling relationships.

Think about just one; one dream of something you'd really like to have in your life but you know you have not done anything to grab onto it.

Okay, now, GO GET IT! Grab it! Do it! Go for it!

—THE END—

Just kidding! Wouldn't it be great if that were all it took?
There's your dream. Go get it! But why isn't it just that simple?
What holds us back when there's something that we really want in
our lives?

Some people believe that what holds us back is a person or people
in our lives. I have a friend, Ed, who is an executive salesman. Ed
earns in the high six figures every year and is, by most people's
standards, very successful. But he's incredibly unhappy. When I
asked him why, he told me that his ex-wife has been "dogging" him,
his kids both have drug problems and his boss won't get off his back.
These people, he says, are keeping him from pursuing his dreams. A
sick parent, an overbearing husband, a wife who doesn't understand
the dedication it takes to achieve our dreams, demanding children, or
an aggravating boss—any of these people in our lives can be a reason
that we are not living our dreams.

For some of us, it's not the people in our lives, but our
circumstances. *"I don't have enough money," "I don't have enough
time," "I don't have enough education," "I have the wrong
education."* We're too old, too young, too short, too tall, too female,
too male, too fat, too thin, too black, too white, too human, or too
Martian.

I don't mean to make light of it. Many people believe that their
circumstances make pursuing their dreams impossible.

But the people and circumstances that we blame for not achieving
our dreams are just *excuses*—not the reasons. When it comes to
pursuing our dreams there are only two things we can be doing:
taking action—or—making excuses. And making excuses is far
easier to do.

"Wait a minute!" I can almost hear some of you saying. *"I have to tend to a sick mother almost every day and I really don't have the time or the energy to pursue anything else right now. At least one person in my life really is holding me back."*

"Yeah!" says another reader. *"I really don't have any money and you need money to start a business. My circumstances are not excuses. They really are holding me back."*

To you poor souls I say take a look at the adversity that some of the people who are living your dreams—doing what you want to do—have overcome and then tell me you're not making excuses.

Helen Keller couldn't see or hear. Her parents were being urged by everyone who knew them to institutionalize her. After all, her life was hopeless. Who would have blamed her for not being able to make anything of it? Such difficult circumstances. But Helen went on to become a world-renown speaker and writer, encouraging millions of people to make more of their lives.

Thomas Edison had a passion for science but he had no formal education. He didn't even finish elementary school, let alone obtain a degree in science or engineering. Who would have blamed him for just accepting the fact that if you have no formal education, you can't grow up to be an inventor and scientist.

Colonel Sanders, the founder of the KFC restaurant chain, closed his small Kentucky restaurant and was penniless when he received his first Social Security check of $105. Starting a new business at age 65, with no money? How could he possibly have succeeded?

And how about Anna Maria Robertson, who started painting in the 1930s at age 78, when arthritis made it impossible for her to continue doing her embroidery. Who would have blamed her if she just lived out her life sitting by a fire in a rocking chair? Instead she became the artist known as Grandma Moses and continued to paint right up until her death at age 101.

Without a doubt, people problems and circumstances can make your effort to live your dreams more difficult and complicated, but they are not the *reason* you don't succeed—just someone or something you can blame. Excuses!

The Fear Factor

The reason we don't live our dreams has to do with an ugly four-letter word that begins with an "F." Don't let your imagination run wild. The word is *FEAR*.

We humans have the capacity to be such spiritual beings, but we spend much of our time as fearful little creatures. We are afraid of EVERYTHING! We're afraid of the big things, like death, disability, disease and disaster, but we're also afraid of things like making decisions, confrontation, answering questions and speaking in public. We're afraid of hundreds of things—and I'm referring to legitimate, ordinary, "lots of people have them" fears. I haven't even given any thought to phobias: Fear of belly button lint. Fear of potatoes. You name it and we can be afraid of it.

We are so fearful it's amazing we can get out of bed in the morning. In fact, I'm convinced that the only reason some of us <u>do</u> get out of bed in the morning is that we're afraid to oversleep. We're afraid we'll lose our jobs or be attacked by dust mites. (If you didn't have this particular fear before, add it to your list).

When it comes to living our dreams, we're afraid of failing, of being embarrassed, of succeeding and having our lives change too rapidly or too dramatically, of being alone, being rejected or being different.

The problem isn't the fear, though. It's how we *respond* to fear. Something we think about or do brings about one or more fear "symptoms." These may include any or all of the following:

A "clenching" or spasm in our "gut"
Pounding, racing heartbeat
Shortness of breath
Dry mouth
Dizziness, loss of balance
Weakness in the legs or knees
Chills, shivering
Shaky hands
Numbness across the chest, shoulders, arms

If fear is present long enough—or intensely enough—we can add many more symptoms: nausea, rash, headache, laryngitis, hiccups— even an overwhelming need to sleep. Increase the intensity or duration even more and you'll have psychosomatic illnesses. If you believe as I do, you know that very real illnesses may not be far behind.

These fear symptoms are usually accompanied by a voice in our heads telling us to stop whatever it is that's causing the fear and to "back off"; warning us of danger or that no good will come of even thinking of taking some kind of action on the dream that gave rise to the symptoms in the first place.

Occasionally, throughout this book, I will be referring to these symptoms collectively as the *fear factor*—a name I was using for them long before the television show of the same name became popular.

We respond to these symptoms, the fear factor, by backing away from whatever is causing them.

So, you met a guy at work who you really like and you dream of being with him. You have his phone number and you decide to take action on your dream. You pick up the phone and start pressing the numbers to call him. As you touch the first button, your hand begins to feel numb. There's a voice in your head—your voice, or maybe your mom's or dad's or a guardian, minister or teacher who influenced you—but it's speaking words you only hear in the presence of fear. It's saying something like this: *"What if he's not interested, my heart would be broken. But he seemed to be interested when we spoke…what if I misread him?"* You punch the second number with a slight hesitation. *"What if he doesn't remember who I am? I'll be mortified."* You tentatively press the third digit. *"What if he doesn't like having women call him?…he thinks I'm too pushy?…he thinks by calling him, I'm too 'easy'?…he has a girlfriend?…he's not interested in women? Maybe it's too late to call. Maybe I'll wait and see if he calls me."* The fear factor is in full bloom, and you hang up the phone, putting an end to the pursuit of your dream.

Or, there's an opening at work that would mean a big promotion for you. Your dream is to have that job. You know you have the skills for it, but you need your boss to put in the good word for you. You decide to talk to him and while you're saying your "good mornings" you realize that he's in a surly mood. Your heart begins to race and you find yourself a little short of breath and dizzy—talking around what you want instead of bringing it out. The voice in your head is telling you to wait. *"This isn't a good time; he's in a lousy mood. He'll tell you you're not good enough, you're not ready. Wait until after lunch."* So you back away. But after lunch there are long distance phone calls and then a rush project and you put if off until tomorrow. Tomorrow, different circumstances seem to prevent the conversation. The next day, it happens again…and the next. Then, you find out that someone else has been given your dream job.

You were afraid, so you stopped and backed off, just as you've done all your life when the fear factor was present. Instead of taking action, you were making excuses. Are you doomed to sabotage your dreams like this for the rest of your life? Do you have serious psychological problems?

Here's the good news. The problem is not a psychological one; it's a problem of education. Your response to fear and the symptoms it brings on is: This *feeling is not okay. I've got to stop and back off.* And for every dream that you're not living and not pursuing, it's always the same.

But here's a news flash:
*** This is a response you <u>learned</u>…***
*** A response that can be unlearned and replaced with a better one.***

Think back to when you were four years old. You gave your Mom a hug on your way out to play in the yard, and she said, *"Goodbye, Honey. Take a lot of risks today! Wander far away from the neighborhood and get really lost so that you can have some adventure and learn to find your way home. Cross a lot of streets by yourself and be sure to talk to lots of strangers—especially if they're looking for a lost puppy or want to offer you candy."* Do you remember?

Of course not—although on a particularly bad day she might have suggested that you go "take a hike" once or twice. Our parents or guardians did their best to stop us anytime they perceived there might be danger.

It's not okay, back away.

You looked into the street from your safe vantage point on the sidewalk and you saw a puddle with an oil slick in it. There were some "cool" colors in that oil slick that you wanted to examine more closely—maybe swirl around with a stick—so you stepped into the street. As your foot touched the blacktop, sirens wailed and alarm bells clanged. No, it was your Mom, yelling, *"Steven, get back on the sidewalk, that's dangerous."* Your heart started to pound—partly because you sensed that fear in her voice of one of the many mysterious dangers only grownups knew about and partly because you were afraid of the disapproving tone. But the fear factor—the racing heart (yours) and the warning voice (hers)—were both there. It wasn't okay to have that feeling, so you had to stop the behavior that caused it and back away.

You found a pencil and wanted to see if it fit into the electrical outlet. As you started to stick it in the receptacle, your father's voice boomed, *"Erica, don't do that. It's dangerous!"* Once again, your heart was racing—the fear symptoms were present and it wasn't okay. You needed to stop and back away.

You wandered down the path a little too far and Mom called out with a sense of urgency that brought you to a halt, *"Joe, stay where Mommy can see you."* Again, that feeling that there might be some danger—or, at the very least, you'd suffer Mom's disapproval—was lurking if you wandered out of the "safe neighborhood" she had defined for you. The safe neighborhood wasn't necessarily a *place*; it could involve *things* (handling knives) and *people* (strangers), as well. You'd do something or go somewhere your guardian thought wasn't safe for you. You'd be warned or scolded or called back and you'd feel fear. Reach up to the stove—your hand would tingle and the word "hot" would be heard—either because Mom said it or, as began to happen, a voice in your own head, called it out. *This isn't okay, back away.*

Eventually, you didn't need your Mom to warn you, to trigger the fear factor and the learned response of stopping some activity. Your own (inner) voice did all the work. *"I better not step in the street or I could get <u>runned</u> over."* [That's not a typo—you were only 4 or 5 years old!]

This response to the fear and the symptoms it produced probably saved your life hundreds of times. It kept you from walking off with strangers, running into the street to chase a ball, burning yourself on hot stoves and wandering away from home to be forever lost. Fear was a good thing, and the "it's not okay, back away" response kept you safe. You learned the limits of your safe neighborhood and a response—backing away—which kept you within those limits.

Welcome to the Neighborhood.

As adults, we still establish a "safe neighborhood," for ourselves. It isn't necessarily a place at all. It's a collection of habits, activities, beliefs, perceptions and attitudes. We create a life for ourselves—a life in large part based on what triggers the fear symptoms and the response to it we were taught. Many people refer to this neighborhood as our *comfort zone*, but some people are so unhappy living in it, that it's often not very comfortable. The boundaries of this safe neighborhood are the places we stop when the fear factor becomes too intense and we need to back off.

There's a woman you think is beautiful. You dream of "sweeping her off her feet." She's popular and is being chased by wealthy, good-looking men. This makes you afraid she won't be interested in a plain guy like you, so you don't approach her. When you try, the fear is so strong that your symptoms include being unable to speak or to say anything remotely intelligent, so you pass her by.

Your dream is to live in California, but you're afraid you'll be too far away from your elderly parents in Chicago and won't be able to afford to jump on a plane and get back to them if they need you. So you take no action on your dream. You back off.

You're in a terrible relationship that you could possibly save, if you only would express how you feel. It's your dream to make it work. But you believe that when you bring up what's bothering you, you'll end up in a fight, or he may even walk out, so you stay where you are, unhappy and doing nothing about it. Dreaming of a relationship you'll never have.

We may be suffering, but our rituals and habits keep us safe from the pain of the fear factor. We're safe if we stay at our present jobs, even if we dream of something different or something that we just know will be better. We stay in relationships that aren't working—dreaming of being somewhere else, but too paralyzed by fear to take action to leave our safe neighborhood.

But when you're an adult with dreams that happen to be beyond that safe neighborhood you've defined for yourself, your learned response to fear—*it's not okay, back away*—is simply <u>inappropriate</u>. As a child, it <u>wasn't</u> okay to be afraid. The fear factor was a warning—a sign that you needed to stop immediately and back off to avoid some danger. Someone should have told you when you were older what I'm telling you now: as an adult desiring to live your dreams, *it IS okay to be afraid*. It's a sign that you are approaching the border of your safe neighborhood, on your way to living your dream. *If this is your dream, you have to just do it—despite the fear.*

> $\mathbf{H}$e who is afraid of a thing gives it power over him.
>
> ~ Moorish Proverb ~

3. The High Diving Board

$\mathbf{F}$ive years after the incident at the theater with Stefanie, I was sitting with a new friend, David, at a sidewalk table at a Chinese restaurant in Princeton. It was a warm summer afternoon. I had been working from my basement office at home and David was between jobs. We had arranged to meet for lunch and talk about what was going on in our lives.

David was fascinated by my story of how I had "transitioned" from a career as a lawyer, which had been making me very unhappy for a long time, to a career as a business seminar leader and corporate trainer. But he was curious about what I wasn't telling him. *"Sandy,"* he asked, *"You've changed your whole life around; started a whole new career and that's something most people don't have the courage to do, but where do you want to go with this—what's your dream?"*

I had known for some time what I wanted to do, but I had not told many people because:

I was afraid they'd think it was foolish,

I was afraid I'd say it and then not do it and feel that I had failed, and

I was afraid I might not be as good at it as I hoped I was.

So, my response was awkward, "sheepish" and almost apologetic.

"Well, I'd love to do what Brian Tracy and Anthony Robbins (two motivational speakers I admired) do. I've come so far in my life and made so many positive changes I think I can really help people learn what I've learned," was the reply. I was even afraid to come out and say what that work was.

"Oh," David responded, *"You want to be a motivational speaker! Well, why don't you just do it?"*

"It's what I really want to do," I started, *"but…"*

There was a lesson coming here—one I had not yet learned about the use of the word "but" and its relationship to making excuses. We'll talk more about it later in this book.

Having uttered the magic word, "but," I had given myself permission to present David with a list of reasons why I wasn't launching myself into the career of my dreams. I didn't realize it then, but I learned a few minutes later that instead of *taking action*, I was *making excuses*.

"I'm not ready, I don't have enough material, I don't know if I'm good enough, I don't know how to start…" I had a long list.

David was good about it, though. He saw my response for what it was, but he didn't challenge me—not yet, anyway. Our conversation turned to summer activities. I told David about a place to which I loved to take my daughters in the summer—a place not far from where we were sitting called The Quarry. An old granite quarry had filled with natural spring water to form an extremely deep lake, surrounded on three sides by high granite walls. The fourth side was open so that swimmers could walk right into the water.

The Quarry has three diving boards. As you approach the water, on your right at ground level is a board that sticks out over the water about a foot and half above the surface. There's always a line at this board—It's right at the lake entrance and the short drop to the water is about the same as you might find at any pool.

On the left, up a small hill, reached by climbing three or four stone steps, is a board that sits about 8 feet above the water. When you jump or dive from this board you have the momentary thrill of the fall. It's just high enough and far enough off to the side that it discourages most of the crowd waiting for the lower board. The third board can make even an experienced diver think twice. It juts out from an opening in the rail of a wooden platform built into the steep cliff wall, about 25 feet above the water. To reach it, you must take a hike on a steep path that begins several yards from the lake entrance and then step out on the platform. It is visited least often, usually by teen boys seeking the thrill of a long "cannonball" jump. Rarely, though, does anyone <u>dive</u> from it.

When I described The Quarry to David, mentioning the three diving boards, he asked me if I liked to dive. I told him that I didn't care much either way for the foot-and-a-half board, with its line of people waiting to use it, but that I liked to dive off the 8-foot board because it was a little more challenging and gave you at least a little thrill when you came off it. I confided in David, however, that one of my dreams was to dive off the 25-foot board, like in an old Tarzan movie where Johnny Weissmuller pounds his chest and dives off the cliff into the Congo River.

"But," I continued, *"I'm irrationally afraid of that board. You'd think after all I've been through—surviving a major automobile accident in which the car tumbled over and over at 60 miles an hour— surviving cancer, two surgeries, chemotherapy and radiation*

therapy—that something like a little diving board where, at worst, I might have some pain from a 'belly flop'—wouldn't phase me."

But I <u>was</u> afraid. Even *thinking* about it made my heart race and made me a little dizzy.

"That sounds a lot like what we were talking about before," David posed. *"When you were talking about your career change,"* he continued, *"you told me that you were unhappy with your career as a lawyer. That career was your foot-and-a-half diving board. So, you became a corporate trainer and seminar speaker. That's your eight-foot board. But what you really wanted to do was to dive off the 25-foot board—to be a motivational speaker. You're just too afraid."*

I started to respond in my defense, but couldn't. I was dumbfounded. David was right. I never went for the high diving board. My *entire life* had been about the eight-foot board. When I graduated college I could have taken a job in a company somewhere, but that would have been the low board. I wanted to be an actor. I went to auditions, did menial work to support myself and spent my small income on acting and singing lessons. But it was too scary to be rejected time after time at auditions and to live on little or no money. I was beyond my safe neighborhood. So I found my eight-foot board. I applied to law school, where even though I had to struggle financially, I could see clear steps to financial security. I was within the borders of my safe neighborhood.

As a lawyer, I was relatively successful. But somehow, I never got to handle that *big* case—the multi-million dollar lawsuit, the million-dollar fee. Was it that these kinds of cases never came my way or that I was too afraid, so that I sent messages that discouraged them? I was willing to do litigation and take on some fairly complex cases—both of which took me beyond the attorneys who stuck to the low board, but I was too afraid to climb the path to the high board.

Here was someone I hardly knew who could see right through my claim that I had been able to overcome my fears; showing me that I had only overcome them to a point that did not take me beyond my safe neighborhood.

All of this flashed through my head in an instant, while I sat there silently absorbing the message, and then I was back at the sidewalk table at the Chinese restaurant in Princeton with David, suddenly perspiring in the warm summer air.

"Sandy," he was saying, *"I'm not a big believer in symbolic gestures, but this one is just too obvious. You've just got to go dive off that board. It's okay to be afraid, because everyone is afraid of something. But this is one of your dreams, and it seems like it is a symbol for some of the others. Even if you're afraid, you just have to go for it!"*

That afternoon, I picked up my daughter Stefanie from her summer theater program and told her we were going to visit The Quarry. I also told her that I intended to dive off the high board. Stefanie was excited about a late afternoon visit to a place we both loved. She told me that even if I change my mind about diving, we could have a good time. There I was, telling her my plan so that it would be harder for me to change my mind and there she was, enabling me to fail, by making it okay to stop and back off. But I knew I couldn't let that happen.

An hour later, Stefanie was floating peacefully on The Quarry lake in a huge black truck inner tube and I was heading up the path that led to the railed wooden platform in the granite cliff wall 25 feet above the water.

I started up the path boldly enough. The voice in my head was chanting, *"It's okay to be afraid. This is your dream, you've got to do it...It's okay to be afraid..."*

The closer I came to the wooden platform, however, the more compelling and aggressive the fear factor became. It showed its face first when my heart started to race and I began having difficulty breathing. Then it was vertigo—dizziness. I swayed a little more than usual with each step and my legs began to feel as if they were made of rubber.

The voice changed, too. The courage mantra, *"It's okay to be afraid..."* was somehow replaced with, *"This is CRAZY! After all you've been through, you don't need to prove anything. You don't have to do this! It makes no sense. You're not a kid, you could get really hurt..."*

Somehow, I reached the platform. There was numbness in my arms as I reached for the support of the rail across the front of the platform--leading to the opening where the diving board jutted out over the water. I gripped it with both hands until my knuckles were white and my arms were shaking involuntarily. My feet—long thin flat ones—attached to a pair of pale skinny legs, suddenly felt like 200-pound boulders that those legs simply couldn't lift. I inched my way along the rail, moving those useless weights ever so slightly to make a step--baby steps. I had to look behind me, because added to my fear of actually going off—or even reaching—the end of the board, was the fear that I looked like a complete idiot! Fortunately, no one was on the platform or coming up the path.

The voice in my head was yelling hysterically now. *"You don't have to do this. You're afraid and you should be."* Somehow I reached the opening and stepped onto the board. Although it was more than a foot wide and extended out about five feet, it seemed as if I had lifted those mighty boulders at the end of my legs onto a long balance beam and was now going to attempt to lift and move them— step-by-step—out to the end of the board, without falling. I held the end of the platform rails on both sides of the board and took the tiniest steps out through the opening into space between them. The voice—"Mom"--was yelling, now. *"Look at those jagged edges on the cliff wall. You'll never reach the end of the board. You're going to lose your balance, go right over the side on your very next step and be smashed to bits on the rocks! Turn back before it's too late!"*

But now there was an argument going on in my head. Another voice was telling me that my fear was understandable, but this is something I've always wanted to do. *"It's okay to be afraid. This is your dream, Tarzan. You're almost there."*

I remembered again, momentarily, my fear of looking like an idiot. I slowly turned my head to assure myself no one was watching. I didn't dare look down to see if Stefanie was watching. Each tiny, agonizingly unsteady step led me further away from the safety of the platform and closer to the end of the board. My heart pounded so hard my chest hurt. I pictured myself lying on the board with a heart attack as one possible way to avoid reaching the end. I swayed uncontrollably and shivered with cold in the 80-degree air, while the voices in my head raged.

Suddenly, I realized that I was now at the end of the board. I hadn't fallen to my eternal suffering on the rocks, or died on the board of heart failure, but I was so paralyzed that I couldn't bring my toes to the edge, as someone does when he's planning to dive. I couldn't move any closer than that last few inches. "Mom" pleaded one more time, *"This is your last chance, turn around!"* And I turned my head back to consider it. But turning around meant moving my right foot to the side and bringing my left foot around—and… I couldn't do it!

When we talk of being paralyzed or frozen, we are often being figurative. This was not the case, at all. I COULDN'T MOVE! There I stood at the end of the 25-foot high diving board, looking at the thimble of lake into which I was supposed to be diving and I couldn't move. I felt as if I was stuck there for hours, but it didn't matter. I would die of starvation in a few weeks at the end of that board, with voices in my head arguing with one another, *"It's okay to be afraid...No, it's <u>not</u> okay, I can't move...but this is your dream...to hell with my dream, I can't move..."*

It occurred to me that I could still sit down and crawl back. But I thought about how miserable I would feel, having come this far and failed to do something so small—something that could break me forever of my "eight-foot board" habit. I leaned forward and...

I hit the water perfectly. Down into the cold darkness and up again. As I broke through the surface into the warm summer air, I tried to act as if this was just another dive of thousands—no big deal. But the smile on my face wouldn't go away and inside, I was yelling, *"YES! YES! YES!"* and dancing in the water.

I realized at that moment how much I had missed, throughout my life, by thinking that the fear factor was my cue to say "I'm afraid and that's not okay," and to stop and back away. All that joy came from saying instead: *"It's okay to be afraid, but this is my dream. Fear or not, I just have to do it."*

I went back to dive again from that platform two more times that day, making sure that it wasn't an accident; that I didn't just fall off the board by mistake that one time. Each time I climbed that path, the fear factor was there, almost as strong as the first time, but I had learned that if it was my dream, I could do it despite the fear. *I had to do it*, despite the fear.

> **C**ourage is not the absence of fear, but rather
> the judgment that something else is more important than fear.
> ~ Ambrose Redmoon ~
>
> **B**ravery is the capacity to perform properly
> even when scared half to death.
> ~ Omar Bradley ~

4. The Truth About Fear And Courage

So, that's it, right? For 20, 30 or more years you've responded to the fear factor by accepting that it's not okay to be afraid—that the fear and its symptoms serve as one big **STOP** sign. You've been responding to the fear factor as you were taught, by stopping and backing away. But now that I've suggested there's a better way to deal with fear, you'll simply start saying: *"It's okay to be afraid, but this is my dream and I have to do it, even if I'm afraid."* Right?

If it were that easy, there'd be no need for books such as this one. Believe me, I know it's not that easy. But I also know that it's not as difficult as you may think. As with anything you've been doing most of your life, learning a new response to your fears will take work and at least a little time, but how much work and how much time, will depend on you.

Even as I lay in my hospital bed after one of my surgeries ten years ago, watching Anthony Robbins' notorious infomercials, I had a burning need to understand why some people are successful and living their dreams and so many are not. Are happy, successful people a myth? If they exist, is it because somehow they were born fearless? If they learned to become fearless, could I learn to become fearless, too? Did you do it by learning to become courageous? Was being courageous living <u>without</u> fear or <u>overcoming</u> fear? Or was it something else?

As I devoted myself to reading motivational books and listening to motivational speakers, I began to understand five truths about fear and courage as they apply to living your dreams:

1. *We will <u>always</u> be afraid of <u>something</u>.* It's human nature. As long as you are alive and growing you will have fears. There are only two kinds of people who don't have fears when it comes to living their dreams: People who have no dreams and dead people. I have come to believe that these two may be one and the same. There are people who <u>believe</u>, as I did, that they have no dreams, because they have become so afraid they can't seem to remember what their dreams are, but they <u>do</u> have dreams. They're just terrified to acknowledge them.

2. *<u>Everyone</u> has fears.* This was a big eye-opener for me: Those happy, successful people are <u>not fearless</u>. They have fears just like everybody else. Often, these fears are of doing the very thing they excel at. Winston Churchill, whose passionate speeches to the British people during World War II are still quoted and remembered, grew up with a severe stutter that made him terrified of public speaking. Barbara Streisand, Wynona Judd and Jennifer Lopez are all petrified

of giving live concert performances, even though they are all incredible performers. What allows them to live the dreams that *we* might want to live—but are *not* living—is that they have somehow learned a new response to their fears. Instead of responding to the fear factor by stopping and backing away—<u>making excuses</u>—they <u>take action</u>. They have been fortunate enough to learn or stumble upon the understanding that it's okay to be afraid when you're pursuing your dreams. But the appropriate response doesn't include stopping and backing away.

Some successful people will tell you they do things <u>because</u> they are afraid. Most know to <u>use</u> the fear—to help them focus and keep them sharp.

3. *Courage is not the <u>absence</u> of fear.* It is taking *action* in the face of fear, instead of backing away. Fear and all those nasty symptoms are a challenge—to expand our "safe neighborhood," no matter how large it may have already grown. It's okay to be afraid, but when you're an adult and the fear is about pursuing your dreams, the childhood response of stopping and backing away is the cowardly response.

Virtually all of the people we call "heroes" who have lived to talk about their heroic deeds will tell you that they were not fearless at the time they took their action. They <u>were</u> afraid, but they used their fear to focus on and take the action they felt needed to be taken.

The heroes of United Flight 93—the plane that crashed near Pittsburgh on September 11, 2001, were undoubtedly afraid, as were the brave firefighters who lost their lives in the World Trade Center collapse. Their heroism does not mean that they were not afraid—only that they took action in the face of their fears.

The passengers on Flight 93 were ordinary people who, without warning, were thrust into a situation where their lives were in serious jeopardy. Their only hope was to mount a counter-attack on the hijackers. They could have simply gone to their deaths quietly, knowing that more innocent people below would die with them, but they didn't want to allow that. Despite their fears, they took action.

The firefighters and police officers overcame fears of placing themselves in dangerous situations even before they chose their professions. But speak to any living fire fighter or police officer and he or she will readily admit that he (or she) is still very much afraid in life-threatening situations. The fear is there. The reaction to that fear is what makes them brave.

Ask anyone decorated for heroism in military action. The answer is almost always the same. *"Yes, I was afraid, but it was something I had to do,"* or *"I was afraid at first, but then I just didn't think about it."*

When it comes to living your dreams, you are not, generally, facing a threat to life or a threat of serious physical injury. I do not recommend pursuing any dream that exposes you or someone else to this kind of threat. But the formula is the same—courage is not fearlessness. It's action in the face of fear.

4. *When you pursue your dreams you can overcome or survive anything that happens.* Fear is a state of mind. Being a product of the mind, it is not necessarily based on realities of the physical world. Almost all of the things we fear don't happen. As

Les Brown says, *"When you face your fear, most of the time you will discover that it was not really such a big threat after all."* Perhaps Mark Twain said it best: *"I have been through some terrible things in my life, some of which actually happened."*

Even the ultimate fear—that we couldn't survive if the very worst happens to us—is an illusion. History is replete with examples of people who have survived and thrived when faced with the worst possible consequences of their pursuits. Yet, we persist in telling ourselves things like:

> *"If I lose all my money, I couldn't take it."*
> *"If he/she walks out on me, I couldn't survive."*
> *"If I have to face my friends after leaving this job, I couldn't handle it."*
> *"If I had to date again, I'd die."*

5. *Once you've experienced what you've been afraid of, you lose some or all of your fear of it.* We invariably find out that once we've faced what we fear, we are less afraid of it the second time. Your safe neighborhood is now a little bigger. My afternoon on the high diving board is proof that this is so. *"Do the thing you fear and keep on doing it,"* Dale Carnegie wrote, *"that's the quickest and surest way ever yet discovered to conquer fear."*

The secretary who dreams of being an actress says, *"I'd never be able to take the rejection."* After being rejected a couple of times, though, she is no longer so afraid of rejection. Her safe neighborhood has grown to include the concept that she <u>can</u> take being rejected. Now, she is afraid she'll <u>always</u> be rejected. Once she gets a small part, she is no longer afraid of she can't take rejection <u>or</u> that she'll always be rejected. At this point, she's afraid she'll never get a <u>decent</u> part.

The recently divorced mother who dreams of finding a relationship with a man better than her last man says, *"I'd just die if I had to start dating again."* After a few dates, though, she is no longer afraid of dating. Her safe neighborhood has grown to include some kinds of dates in some circumstances. She may be afraid that she won't find someone who is right for her, or of something else, and she may not like dating, but she no longer believes she couldn't do it at all.

And so it goes. One fear subsides and new ones appear.

I hope by now you at least see that what I'm saying here is true. Throughout the rest of this book, we'll be exploring how to recognize when you're afraid, and when you're making excuses instead of taking action. We'll examine how to teach yourself the adult response: to understand that it's okay to be afraid, but that it's not okay to react by backing way—you just have to do it!

> **A** life worth living is worth writing about.
>
> ~Anonymous~

5. Ten Steps to Living Your Dreams

Step One: Put it in writing.

Congratulations! You're at The Quarry. You're standing outside the audition room. You wanted a change in your life badly enough to find and buy this book and to read it to this point.

But are you ready to start climbing the path to your high diving board? Because that's where we're going.

How do you know you're ready? You're willing to put it in writing.

Having read a majority of the motivational books written since the 1850s and listened to hundreds of recorded and live motivational talks, I am convinced of the importance of writing things down: writing out goals and dreams; keeping a journal (or several of them); writing out positive affirmations; etc.

But one of the hardest things for me to do was to write about my deepest thoughts—dreams and fears. It is a major commitment that frightens most of us. It gives our fleeting thoughts permanence and importance and makes us vulnerable to the possibility that even if we keep our writings well hidden, someone might discover them. If they do, they'll learn that the façade we present to the world may not be who we really are. So, we do what we always did—we back away.

If you want to live your dreams, though, there's no doubt that the commitment to write about them and about the fears that hold you back is the first step you need to take.

Commit to keeping a journal. Keep several journals for different purposes, if you wish. One might be used to record daily events. Another might be for scribbling dreams, hopes, wishes, desires, and inner secrets. You might keep a "success" journal, where you write your goals and record your progress in reaching them. In this journal, record each day some step you took toward reaching your goals and one or two you promise yourself for tomorrow.

Or, you might simply keep everything in one journal. Try to write in your journal every day, but if you can't, do it as often as you can. Even once each month is better than not at all.

Copy and write down quotations and sayings that inspire you. Put them everywhere—at your desk at work, on your refrigerator, at your desk at home, and on your bathroom mirror.

One very successful salesman I work with writes down the inspirational quotations he finds and tapes them to his steering wheel to read over and over again on his way to appointments. From a safety standpoint, I don't recommend this particular practice, but it gives you an idea of how creative you can be.

For our work on your dreams, you will be guiding yourself along with the written exercises in the coming chapters. If you haven't yet developed the habit of keeping a journal, *BUT* you don't even have a sheet of paper, have no fear—I believe so strongly in the power of the written word as an aid to changing your life that I've packaged a *Dream Journal* with this book. All you need to find is a pen or pencil. (*"But* I can't find a pen...").

Take a look at the *Dream Journal* I have supplied at the end of this book, beginning on page 117. The very first thing you are asked to do on page 118 is to commit, *in writing*, to making your dreams come true. Make this commitment by reading, signing and dating it—creating a contract with yourself (I told you I was a lawyer, didn't I?) and you're ready to start creating a better life for yourself. Let's get to those dreams of yours...WADDAYAWANT?

No one will blame you if you can't take this first step on the path. Your learned response to fear has been a dominant force in almost every important life decision you've made. Maybe you just have to put this book away until, someday, you are ready. But before you do—before you give up—read the next chapter. Maybe it will help.

> **I** *know* what you should be doing.
>
> You should be doing what you love.
>
> ~Barbara Sher~

Step Two: Remember your dreams.

At this point, you've either taken Step One and made the commitment to climb the path to your High Diving Board—wherever it's leading—or you haven't. If you haven't made the commitment yet, I'm going to let you off the hook if you promise to at least keep on reading the next few chapters.

As with any journey, you need to have some idea where you're going. And as with everything we will be doing, the best way to make it clear is to write it out. At the end of this chapter, I'll be asking you to write down in your *Dream Journal* three of the dreams you haven't been pursuing. You can always find paper or another journal and write down more.

"But I don't know what my dreams are," you might be saying, *"I'm unhappy, but maybe I just don't have any dreams."* Of course, you can't pursue your dreams if you don't even know what they are.

At age four or five, there was probably something that you were brilliant at and passionate about. Maybe your special talent was bugs. You knew the name of every insect in the universe and you had your own system of cataloging them—by size, number of legs and wings— a system that might have become the standard of today. Or maybe you loved plants. You spoke to them and they spoke to you. They told you their problems and you helped them solve them. Or you were a musical theater genius. You produced and directed hundreds of amazing extravaganzas starring Hollywood Barbie and the Beanie Babies. Somehow, though, you now can't remember what your passion and your special talent were. What happened?

There was Mom, constantly calling you away from your life's passion to do something she wanted you to do and your teachers, doing their best to "socialize" you.

Imagine a first grade classroom with three exceptional students: Albert Einstein, Pablo Picasso, and Wolfgang Amadeus Mozart.

The teacher, Miss Crabtree, has called everyone to the circle for story time, but Albert sits over near the window, examining the patches of bright sunlight on the dusty wooden floor. Pablo is busy drawing with crayons on a big sheet of newsprint and Wolfgang is developing a symphony on the old classroom piano.

Miss Crabtree is waiting and growing impatient. Finally, she calls out with obvious irritation, *"Albert! Albert Einstein! I know you're probably trying to figure out how fast the sunlight is moving, but it's story time and everyone is waiting for you. Please speed your way over here this minute."*

She turns to young Mozart. *"Wolfgang Amadeus! Will you please stop banging on that piano and come join us for story time. Everyone is waiting for you."*

Little Picasso is tugging at the hem of her skirt, trying to get her attention. *"What's that Pablo?"* she asks. He shows her his drawing. *"That's a very nice drawing, Pablo. But does your mommy really have two faces like that? Next time, try to draw her facing in one direction only, okay?"*

And if the adults did what they thought their jobs were right, you forgot what it was you were passionate about. Your "amnesia," as Barbara Sher calls it in her book, *Wishcraft*, started with being afraid that your particular "something" was the *wrong* thing; that you wouldn't get the attention and praise you need—or worse—that you'd be criticized for it. It became something that was beyond the borders of your safe neighborhood. Since you were also learning to respond to fear by backing away, that's what you did about those "somethings" which delighted you. You backed away from them.

You grew up and took a job in some field you—or circumstances—chose. Maybe you even became very good at what you do. If you're one of those rare lucky people, you picked something about which you were passionate. If not, you live with an empty feeling: the feeling that you don't know what you want; the feeling that you've forgotten something. And you have. You've forgotten what it was you were passionate about, what gave you a sense of fulfillment.

The same thing happened at other points in your life and with other aspects of it—with your choice of friends, with your choice of a partner and in your relationships with family, friends and everyone else. Your fears sent you in a direction that cut you off from the "somethings" about which you were passionate, and you developed amnesia about them.

But you didn't really forget. Every once in awhile, in some quiet moment, one of these passions crosses your mind or finds its way to your heart. At that moment, however, instead of embracing it, you back away. It's too scary to think about!

Trust that if you're a living human being, you <u>do</u> have dreams. You just need to *remember* them. When I was unhappiest as a lawyer, my paralyzed response to my fears had caused me to push my dreams down so deep inside me that I actually believed that I didn't have any —beyond the dream of not practicing law. I was one of the many people who had become so afraid of stepping beyond the borders of my safe neighborhood, that I made myself believe that I had no dreams—no reasons to ever do it. I didn't have a clue what I wanted to do instead of being a lawyer. The answer to *"WADDAYAWANT?"* was *"I don't know."*

The fear factor pounced on me even when I was just *thinking* about what I *might* like to do with my life instead of being a lawyer. What can you do when you're so afraid that you tremble from just <u>thinking</u> about what your dreams might be?

Maybe there are people who truly don't know what they want, but most who say they don't know, really do. Their fears are so strong, they can't bring themselves to say the words.

For several years before my illness, as the dreams I once had were disappearing, I lived as a Zombie, trapped in my safe neighborhood and going through the motions of living. I woke up, went to work, came home, went to sleep and started the next day. The only time my light would shine was when I was spending time with my children. I was chronically depressed—imprisoned in a life that held no adventure, no joy (except for what my girls brought me), no passion and no sense of fulfillment. Is it any wonder that my body showed virtually no resistance to a potentially fatal illness?

As I stood in the hallway of the theater basement with Stefanie, barely functioning as a human being, I was happy for her that she at least knew what her dreams were.

When had I "lost" mine? I was so deeply depressed, I came to believe that dying would not be such a bad thing. After all, I had a large insurance policy, so I was obviously worth more to my family dead than not quite alive.

As my sense that my death was imminent subsided and my disability improved, instead of finding joy in the fact that I could live and function again, I grew even more depressed. *"If I hate what I'm doing but have no idea of what I'd like to do, what's left for me?"* I would think. I looked down the road and all I could see was sixty hours a week of adventureless, joyless, passionless, unfulfilling work, followed by death. What was the point?

I read every motivational book I could find. I listened to every motivational tape. I spent hundreds of dollars I didn't have and hundreds of hours reading, searching for a way to help myself out of my dilemma and my depression. Then, a friend recommended two books which helped me understand that I really *did* know what I wanted—that I had always known. These books started me on a study and practice of courage that has changed the course of my life: *Feel the Fear and Do It Anyway*, by Susan Jeffers, and *I Could Do Anything If I Only Knew What It Was*, by Barbara Sher.

The message of these authors wasn't necessarily new, but they provided me with the first steps on my road to a better life; my first lessons in courage:

- Every one of us really knows what we want; what our dreams are. They are the "somethings" that make us smile, make us passionate, give us a sense of adventure, and bring joy and a sense of fulfillment to our lives. They are different for each of us but each of us has them.

- If you can't find yours, it's most likely because you're afraid: that you might have to make changes in your life and risk leaving your safe neighborhood if you even acknowledge them; that you might pursue them and have to deal with the consequences of change; or that you might be too afraid to pursue them and that would be more painful than simply never acknowledging them.

If you truly want to find your lost dreams, start with this Preliminary Exercise:

PRELIMINARY EXERCISES. (For anyone who thinks he or she has no dreams or can't find them. If you know you have dreams and know what they are, these preliminary exercises are optional). Turn to your Dream Journal. Even if you haven't made the commitment at the beginning, take a chance that I know what I'm talking about by starting with these exercises:

(1) With your Dream Journal in hand, open to pages 119-125 and find a quiet place to sit and think about all the things that gave you joy at different times in your life. What were your passions when you were a child: Dinosaurs? Puppet shows? The stars? Your best friend Randy? What happened to those passions? [Don't write, "I grew out of them"! That's probably not what really happened.] What about when you were a teenager? How about after high

*school—college or work or both? Who were the friends,
boyfriends, girlfriends who made you smile and what
happened to them? What about them made you smile? Write
down your thoughts and you should begin to see that there
are things you wish you had in your life now. Hey, these are
dreams!*

(2) Ask yourself these questions to jog your memory:

With what about my life am I least happy?

What do I most want that I don't have already?

What would I like my life to look like a year from now?

In two years?

In five years?

In ten years?

In twenty years?

How do I feel about…

- *My relationships?*
- *My income?*
- *My work?*
- *My education?*
- *My spiritual life?*

*These kinds of questions should help to remind you what your
dreams are.*

*(3) What is it that you don't like about the situation you're in
right now? Write down as many things as you can think of.
Are you happy with your work? What is it you don't like about
it? Are you happy with your relationships—the "significant
other" situation, your family situation, friends? What don't
you like about any or all of these?   How about your free time?*

Do you have any? Do you have too much or too little? What about your free time don't you like? How about your home? Your neighborhood? Your community?

Once you have a list of all of the things you don't like about your life, you can simply "turn it around." If you don't like your working conditions, you dream of better working conditions. If you're not happy with your "significant other," your dream is to improve that relationship—or end it and find another—or just to end it, without even thinking about another. Once again, you've found your dreams.

Still stuck? There's another way to remember your dreams…*Take action*. Do something—any small thing—which leads you in a direction that seems interesting to you. Do hundreds of small things in every direction that appeals to you.   The key is in taking action—*any action*—other than making excuses and complaining how miserable your life is. Any small step will start you on the road to joy.

Taking action instead of making excuses! One small step each day, in any direction, you *might* want to go. As many possible dreams as you can fit in each day. As many small steps for each dream that you can take without being overwhelmed by your fear factor.

There was a point in my life when I was doing <u>all</u> of the following at the same time:

- *Part-time legal work*
- *Part-time work in the management of my wife's retail business*
- *Sending resumes for business law teaching positions*

*   *Sending resumes for business startup and management teaching positions*
*   *Sending resumes for corporate training positions*
*   *Part-time small business consulting and coaching*
*   *Part-time work as the Executive Director of a small non-profit association*
*   *Developing, marketing and presenting business seminars whenever I could*

I was also spending time with family and friends and looking for a way to satisfy my "spiritual" side. I worked hard to get it all in. There's an amazing phenomenon that occurs when you are working to or beyond your capacity. You can do more than you ever dreamed. People who are out of work for awhile may take an entire day to clean the leaves out of the gutters of their home. Give them two full-time jobs and the likelihood is that they will still somehow find time to get the gutters cleaned.

And all it took to pull me out of my deep depression and "find" my dreams was some small positive action each day: sending out a resume or two; reading a chapter in a book on a topic for which I thought I might like to create a seminar; or working on a speech for Toastmasters, where I practice my speaking skills and build my confidence.

When you've figured out at least three of your dreams, you're ready for your first dream-building exercise. So, *WADDAYAWANT?*

EXERCISE 1. Find a quiet place (again) and let your mind run wild. Write down three of your dreams on the lines provided

on page 125 in your Dream Journal. Then write each dream
again—one at the top of each of the next few pages to the right
of the heading—"My Dream." Don't edit or censor your
dreams (except to the extent that there is a real danger to
someone—like bungee jumping without a bungee cord or
shooting at passing cars). It doesn't matter if it appears
impossible on the surface. If you're a 72 year-old woman who
stopped working the line at the auto plant seven years ago after
putting in 25 years; and you dream of going to medical school
to become a brain surgeon or of having Brad Pitt fall madly in
love with you and asking you to marry him, write it down.
Dare to dream and write your dreams down. They may
change, or you may think of others, but capture them as they
come to you now.

While I have given you space for three dreams in the *Dream Journal*, I did not mean for you to stop at three. You can start with three or get some paper and write more. Write out all of the dreams you can think of at the moment. When you are satisfied that living these particular dreams will give you all the joy you deserve, put your *Dream Journal* (or your list—or both, if you've used both) somewhere where you can look at it every day.

In his book, *The Seven Spiritual Laws of Success*, Deepak Chopra suggests that you make this promise to yourself:

"I will make a list of my desires. I will carry the list with me wherever I go. I will look at this list before I go into my silence and meditation. I will look at it before I go to bed at night. I will look at it when I wake up in the morning."

> $\mathbf{A}$s long as you do not violate the other laws of nature,
> through your intent you can literally command the laws of nature
> to fulfill your dreams and desires.
>
> ~Deepak Chopra~

Step Three: Explore the underlying dreams.

I tell people not to edit their dreams; that they can have anything their hearts truly desire. I always add an exception, of course, for those dark dreams that may endanger their lives or well being or the lives or well being of others.

Invariably, however, someone says, *"Wait a minute. I'd like to be 18 again. I can dream that all I want but it is never going to happen."* Or, *"My dream is to be a professional basketball player. I'm 5'2" tall, weigh 210 pounds and I'm 57 years old. And besides, I'm lousy at basketball and haven't played in years. I don't care what you say, my dream is never going to come true—even if I'm the most courageous person in the world."*

In a sense, these people are right. Even I can't fulfill the dream of being 18 again chronologically—it violates the laws of nature. It would probably make sense to add another exception; to say that you can have anything you dream of *that doesn't violate the laws of nature,* but dreams sometimes <u>do</u> violate the laws of nature. (*"Sorry Wilbur and Orville Wright, a machine heavier than air will simply never fly—it violates the laws of nature!"*) Another marvel about dreams is that often they serve as *symbols* for what we <u>really</u> want.

Anthony Robbins asks, *"When we say we want lots of money, are we saying that what we really want is little green pieces of paper with pictures of dead people on them?"* What we may really want is some *aspect* of the thing we're dreaming about, or the *feeling* we think we'll get from having it.

Two people may both be dreaming about having great wealth. To one, having that kind of money means never having to worry about being hungry or cold, while the other may be dreaming that he can afford to travel extensively, live in mansions and have jewels and luxury cars. Neither really cares about having those little green pieces of paper. If you dream of being outrageously rich, do you really need to have millions of dollars, or is it that you want to be able to travel the world and being rich is the one way you thought you could do that? If the latter is true, is there another way to travel around the world?

Maybe I can never be eighteen again, but I can dream that I put myself into the physical shape I was in when I was 18—give or take a few unavoidable consequences of nature. I could start listening to the music that 18-year olds listen to and be the oldest fan at the concerts they go to. I could act like an 18-year old and wear the clothes that 18-year olds wear and find myself being looked at oddly by both 18-year olds and people my own age. I could watch what they like to watch on television and go to movies they like. Or, I could become a counselor to young adults. Or, I could just become Dick Clark and live forever.

One or more of these things might be what I'm really dreaming of, if I'm dreaming of being 18 again. For this reason, among others, we should never dismiss our dreams as impossible.

Two young men may both dream of becoming successful actors. For one, that dream means being famous, having adoring fans, money and privilege. The other may view success as an actor as perfecting his craft, learning from the masters and having an opportunity to be steadily employed in the field he loves.

Our 57-year old basketball pro may not need to actually sit on the Lakers bench. He may want a job working closely with professional basketball or he may be satisfied to spend a week at a "Basketball Fantasy Camp" where he can actually play the game with some current or retired pros. Or, maybe he <u>does</u> just want to sit on that bench in the arena—whether the team's there or not.

Now that you've written your dreams down, look at them to see what feeling you are looking for that you're not getting now— security, peace, creature comforts, the ability to give more, being appreciated. If you wrote down a dream like being fabulously rich or having a handsome prince bring you a glass slipper, rewrite it, focusing on what you <u>really</u> want. Here's an exercise that will help you do that:

EXERCISE 2. Starting on page 126 of your Dream Journal, in the area for each dream under the heading "My dream refined" write the specific things about that dream that you really want.

Are you interested in brain surgery because you want to help people, or you want to study the brain, or you would like to make the kind of money a surgeon makes, or because you'd like to work in a hospital? Is it all of those things or will one or two of them satisfy you? I leave the possible questions in the Brad Pitt marriage proposal example to your imagination.

> Are you living your dreams?
> If the answer is no, then I ask "why not?"
>
> Life is short, and you never know when it will come to an end.
> Do you really want to say that you lived
> a life of unfulfilled dreams?
>
> ~ Deborah Brown ~

Step Four: Feel your pain.

Have you signed the commitment at the beginning of the *Dream Journal* yet? Let's take a look at what you have now and what you could have if you committed to those changes in your life you're afraid to make.

Even if you <u>have</u> made the commitment, it wouldn't hurt to have a better understanding of the significance of your commitment.

Short of a threat to your life, or being in a position where you know you're exposed to that kind of threat, what can make you take action on your dreams?

One theory is that nothing will—that you won't make any changes without significant pain.

In his *"Personal Power"* series, Anthony Robbins discusses at length a basic principle about which psychologists have been aware for decades: Most *of us will change our lives only when we perceive it is less painful to change than it is to stay where we are.*

The theory is that we humans respond to the world around us in much the same way that most creatures do: we seek pleasure and try to avoid pain. Given a choice of the two, the avoidance of pain is always the more powerful motivator.

When it comes to change of any kind, we tend to seek what psychologists and biologists call "homeostasis"—a "drive-free" condition. When we are hungry, we are motivated to reduce that drive by eating. When we feel pain, we are motivated to reduce that drive by moving away from the source of the pain. Whenever a drive is unsatisfied, we are aroused to make a change, but faced with a perception that the process of change will be painful, we don't do it. We're prisoners in our own "safe neighborhood."

But our safe neighborhood is not the place about which we dream. We're not doing the work we know we were meant to do; we're not in the loving relationships we believe we could have; or, we're not happy with our physical appearance, our habits, or some other aspect of our lives. To have what we dream will make our lives better, we need to wander <u>outside</u> our safe neighborhood. We <u>need to do things that make us afraid</u> and expose us to the fear factor.

Let's face it, though, the fear factor—that collection of fear symptoms about which we've been talking—is painful. The symptoms bring us actual physical pain and more fear—anxiety—stress. We want to fulfill our dreams, but it's so much more "comfortable" to stay in the place where our dreams are not being fulfilled. You know what you can expect here in your safe neighborhood. You know the places that make you afraid and you've learned ways to keep away from them.

You know you need to "network" to make your dream career a reality, but you're afraid of meeting new people, so you avoid organizations that might benefit your career. You dream of meeting someone you can share your life with, a dream that involves social situations, but parties and other gatherings make you nervous, so you make excuses not to go. You dream of finally saying what you need to say to your boss (your "significant other," a family member, a friend) but you're afraid of confrontation, so you don't do it.

Why would you move toward your dreams if you perceive that doing so could be more painful than staying where you are—no matter how unhappy you might be where you are?

If we accept the "pain controls action" principle as true, changing our response to fear when it pops up in the course of pursuing our dreams—becoming *courageous* instead of *paralyzed*—can only happen if there is a change in our perception of which life is more painful. Is it the one where we never live our dreams, but never face the fear factor? Or, is it the one in which we face the fear factor and live the life we want to live?

We need to somehow perceive that it is more painful to stay in our safe neighborhood for life than to attempt to do something that takes us beyond its boundaries. *In other words, we need to feel that it is more painful to keep making excuses than it would be to take action.*

How painful would it be to never have those things—that life— about which you dream...to live out the rest of your life wishing that you had at least tried...wondering how it might have been if you had?

I had been a lawyer—work I hated for at least the last five of the fifteen years I was in full-time practice, even though my business continued to grow and people praised my work. I was surrounded by other lawyers who felt the same way. They dreamed of being elsewhere—doing something else with their lives—but none of them did anything about their dreams. Instead of *taking action* to make their lives better and pursuing their dreams, they *made excuses*:

"I hate this, but where else am I going to make this kind of money?"

"I don't know how to do anything else."

Year after year, I'd express my unhappiness to friends and family members and listen to those same lawyers as they expressed their pain. BUT...there were mortgage payments and car payments and kitchens that needed remodeling and credit card debt from overspending and sorely needed vacations and all those things that needed to be paid for. How else *would* we get the money? And what else *could* I do? Certainly, *my* circumstances made it impossible for me to take any action to change. Didn't they?

Finding a career that wasn't about long hours, mountains of paperwork, hundreds of phone calls, each bringing with it some kind of aggravation, arguments with everyone about everything and battles—often with my own clients who were satisfied with the work but couldn't understand why they had to pay for it—was certainly a great dream. But as painful as staying where I was might have been, my perception—and the perception of these other lawyers—was that leaving our safe neighborhood to do something new was even more painful.

Although many people have congratulated me for having had the courage to change careers after spending years building a successful law practice, the truth is that it took very little courage. It simply became more painful to stay in the profession I hated than it was to launch myself into the unknown beyond its boundaries.

In 1992, we learned I had cancer. The news came a few weeks after a terrible automobile accident in which the car I had been driving tumbled over and over at 60 miles per hour nearly resulting in my death and the death of my daughters. What followed the devastating cancer pronouncement was a year of surgeries, several hospitalizations, chemotherapy and radiation therapy, leaving me totally disabled for several months. Most of my clients had to find other lawyers, since I was unavailable.

When I had recovered sufficiently to work again, I was faced with the prospect of rebuilding my practice—expending great quantities of time, energy and emotion prospecting for work I hated—or finding something new. Rebuilding was much more painful than changing. So, I took action on my dreams despite my fear.

But I don't recommend this kind of motivation. And, as powerful as it was, it didn't take me all the way to where I wanted to be—to my high diving board, my dream career. It only took me as far as the eight-foot board. Once my health crisis appeared to have passed and my physical suffering and fear of imminent death were no longer motivational forces, I needed to find a new driving force to give me the "courage" to continue exploring beyond my "8-foot" safe neighborhood.

Specifically, my challenge was to find a way to associate enough pain with responding to my fears the old way, that I would find it less painful to climb up the path to that high diving board than to stay in my new safe neighborhood.

In the course of my research on overcoming my fears I discovered an exercise that helped me see how much pain there would be if I gave into my fears and didn't take action on my dreams. It's an exercise that takes all of ten minutes and then provides you with a tool you can keep on using:

EXERCISE 3. Feel the pain. Beginning once again on page 126, for each dream that you refined in Exercise 2, in the areas provided in your Dream Journal, write about all of the pleasure you'll have if you actually pursue and attain your dream. Take about five minutes on each dream. Then, take another five minutes to write, in as much detail as possible, in the "pain area" about all of the pain you'll suffer if you never even try to pursue your dream.

Here's a sample of what mine looked like:

BECOMING A MOTIVATIONAL SPEAKER AND WRITER
The pleasure I'll feel if I do it

I'll have the pleasure of knowing that I chose my own direction and had the strength and courage to persist until I reached my goal. I'll feel truly successful and fulfilled. I'll get up every day looking forward to the work I have ahead of me, having a sense that I really make a difference in this world and in the lives of people I touch. I'll meet people all over the country, maybe all over the world and share ideas and the joy of life with them and I'll learn from them while I'm giving them something they want and need. I'll have the money I want so I can stop worrying about it and truly enjoy each day, doing what I want to do without worrying about whether it's helping to pay the bills...

> ### *BECOMING A MOTIVATIONAL SPEAKER AND WRITER*
> #### *The pain I'll suffer if I don't do it*
>
> *I'll know that I never really lived my life; that I let fear hold me back from doing what I wanted to do and was capable of doing. I'll never get over the debt we've accumulated since my illness and will die still owing people—including friends and family—money. I'll see people living my dream, the motivational speakers of tomorrow, and will feel jealousy and envy, knowing that I could have at least <u>tried</u> to do what they do but was too cowardly. I'll feel that I didn't make enough of a difference; didn't help all of the people I might have helped; didn't even help myself to be successful. I'll feel I was a <u>failure</u> and I'll feel guilty that this was the best example I could give my daughters...*

If you're one of those people who hasn't yet made the commitment to go after your dreams, are you ready now? If you are committed, can you feel how much more painful it will be to continue playing it safe than to go after your dreams?

Let's move on to the next step—identifying just what it is that you are afraid of...

What is there to be afraid of?
The worst thing that can happen is you fail. So what?
I failed at a lot of things. My first record was horrible.

~John Mellencamp~

You may be disappointed if you fail,
but you are doomed if you don't try.
~Beverly Sills~

The next best thing to winning is losing!
At least you've been in the race.

~Nellie Hershey Smith~

Step Five: Identify what it is you're afraid of.

If you've done the exercises to this point, you should now be able to look down at your Dream Journal and see your dreams, refined so that what you want in your life is staring back at you. You should also have a sense of the joy you'll have in your life if you pursue those dreams and how miserably painful it will be if you don't pursue them because you are afraid.

But fear is a powerful force and simply deciding that you're going to "do it anyway" doesn't necessarily get you started. Your mind is saying, *"Yes, Sandy, I agree that it's okay to be afraid and that if this is my dream I have to take action anyway, despite the fear—in my head—BUT—I'm still too afraid to move. The rest of me hasn't caught up with my head. I just can't get myself to pick up that phone—to take action."*

You know you need to take action, but you simply can't.

What are we afraid of? Assuming our dreams don't involve a real risk of death, disfigurement or disability to us or anyone else, what if we try and it doesn't work out?

In October of 1993, Michael Jordan left basketball and took up baseball. The whole world saw that it didn't work out. In 2001, he was back playing basketball. Despite his fame as a basketball player, he knew that he'd never be truly happy unless he at least tried to excel in another sport. And try he did, but he didn't excel.

Trying and failing doesn't mean you can't make it. It just means that it's hard to succeed. If it were easy, <u>everyone</u> would be doing it.

If we don't make it when we reach for one of our dreams, we can usually find a way to move back to our old safe neighborhood, but even if, for some reason, we truly couldn't go back, we can create <u>new</u> safe neighborhoods. Why won't we just let ourselves believe that?

In my own journey to overcome fear, I found it helpful to take a look at the fears that paralyze most people; to see what they're really about and to determine which ones were holding me back. Let's do that together now.

When it comes to pursuing our dreams, we usually experience one or more of the *Seven Paralyzing Fears*. We can be afraid of <u>all</u> of them at the same time:

THE SEVEN *PARALYZING* FEARS

1. Fear of failing.
2. Fear of being embarrassed.
3. Fear of making a mistake—of committing to the wrong thing.
4. Fear of being rejected/alone/an outcast.
5. Fear of climbing too high; that we don't deserve our dreams; we're not worthy.
6. Fear that we're not ready, not capable, or inadequate.
7. Fear of success.

1. Fear of failing. This is one of the first fears people acknowledge. It is closely tied to the fear of being embarrassed. Most of us would not mind reaching for one of our dreams and not being able to attain it, *if no one else knew about it.* We fear that we'll wake up one morning, go to the mirror and see the word "LOSER" printed across our foreheads in permanent black marker. When we go out on the street, *everyone* will see it and know.

"There goes Tom. He left a perfectly good job to open a business of his own and it failed. He lost all his money, and everybody knows it."

"Look, there's Sherry. She thought she was unhappy with her relationship, so she confronted her boyfriend about the things she wanted to improve and he dumped her. Now, she's alone, and everybody knows it."

"There's Rob. He told his boss that he deserved a bigger pay raise and a promotion and the company let him go. Now, he's out of work, and everybody knows it."

So what if you've "failed" in the eyes of other people? Nobody died and no one has suffered permanent physical injury. And you were pursuing your dreams. Can any of those other people say that?

"But people will know and they'll talk about me," you might say. *"Everyone will know I'm a failure. How will I be able to show my face in public again?"*

There's an old adage that almost every self-made millionaire has been totally broke at least once or twice before succeeding. Artists starved. Inventions blew up.

Thomas Edison had this wacky dream that he could create a viable light source from—of all things—electricity. He initiated *thousands* of experiments with different materials and combinations of materials to find something that would glow brightly enough, without bursting into flames, exploding or melting, to serve as a useful alternative to candelabras, oil lamps and gas chandeliers.

He held the wire leads from an electrical source on the ends of a pencil and wrote in his notebook: *"pencil—no response."* He put the leads into a pan of water and wrote, *"pan of water—bubbles."* He put the pencil in the water, held the leads in the pan and wrote *"pencil in water—more bubbles."* Then, he put his cat in the pan and brought the leads to the water, and—Oops! Never mind the cat.

Edison met with one "failure" after another until he stumbled upon the right combination: a thin wire coil in a vacuum tube. He had invented the light bulb. A hundred years later, most of our light still comes from bulbs made more or less the same way as the one he created in his laboratory.

A young reporter interviewing the now very successful inventor was curious how he could have failed so many times—thousands of times--and kept on going.

Edison was incredulous. *"Young man,"* he reportedly replied, *"I never failed; I simply learned five thousand ways it didn't work."*

Edison knew instinctively something most of us have to be taught:

There is no failure—except the failure to try.

It was exciting to watch Mark McGuire hit 70 home runs in 1998. He also struck out 155 times that year. Mark had, at the time of his 70th, hit 457 home runs during his career, but he had also struck out 1,259 times. Imagine if he thought having so many strikeouts made him a failure.

How about Michael Jordan? His career shooting average is about *fifty percent.* Imagine anyone thinking that Jordan is a failure because he misses half his shots.

If you learn something from your experience, you haven't failed. The people who would make you think you are a failure are people who *have* failed—they have dreams they are too paralyzed to pursue.

2. *Fear of being embarrassed.* To fear being embarrassed, you don't even have to <u>try</u> what you're dreaming about. Imagine the 6-foot 4-inch 250-pound football player who dreams of learning ballet. It doesn't matter whether it turns out that he's terrific at it—narrow-minded people will laugh at anyone's attempt to live his or her dreams. These are, however, usually people who have never tried—

and are too afraid—to live their own dreams. They don't want you to succeed; because it will prove that being courageous works.

People laughed at Christopher Columbus, Susan B. Anthony, the Wright brothers, Thomas Edison, and Albert Einstein, to name a very few.

Walt Disney was already a famous cartoonist when he dreamed of opening an amusement park that would feature his cartoon characters. People he respected—bankers and venture capitalists laughed at him. Isn't it grand that he didn't listen to them?

Harland Sanders of Kentucky was 65 years old and penniless when he decided to try to turn his chicken recipe into a franchise business. People laughed at him, too! None of them could have guessed that he had just begun KFC, one of the largest food franchises in world.

Yet, our fear that people might laugh at the sight of us stumbling along as we pursue our dreams keeps us from living them— particularly if we're 6-foot 4-inch football players in tights.

Sitting at the sidewalk table on that sunny summer day, when David asked me what my dream was, I was too embarrassed even to say it; too afraid that I'd be laughed at to even utter the words. Today, it's rare that I would get embarrassed about pursuing my dreams, because when you pursue them, they can come true. Remember the Colonel.

3. *Fear that we'll make a mistake; we'll make the wrong decision and be committed to it*.

Here's another news flash:

*There are **no wrong decisions**!*

In the 1960s and 70s, there was a hugely popular television game show called "Let's Make A Deal." The host, Monty Hall, would go out into the audience, hand someone a $20 bill and tell her she can either keep it, or trade it for whatever is in the box he or an assistant was holding. Everyone knew that what was in the box could be totally useless—a can of cat food—or something wonderful, like two tickets to Hawaii. If the contestant took the box, he'd hold off showing her what was in it and offer her what was behind one of the curtains up on the stage or behind the stage door. Once again, what was on the stage could be a mule and a bale of hay or a shiny new car. You never would know.

People loved this game. They were so crazy about it that it was impossible to get tickets to be in that studio audience. People who did get tickets to a show began dressing in outrageous costumes to attract Monty's attention. You and a friend might go to the show dressed as a tube of toothpaste and a roll of toilet paper or as two ends of a horse. You'd be hoping for the chance to be selected as an audience contestant, and happy no matter how it turned out.

If, for instance, you ended up making a bad trade and going home with the can of cat food, you'd display it on your living room coffee table and tell the story to all your friends. How much better to win the trip to Hawaii? But it didn't matter either way. There were no wrong decisions—and that's why people loved the show.

It was a contrast, they believed, to real life, where a wrong decision could send you irrevocably down the wrong path. Do you ruin a "good" career—the one in the box—that isn't the career of your dreams—to chase after one behind the curtain? Or do you stay (in the box) and let the dream career go by? What if you chose the curtain and the box was better? End the relationship in the box with someone who cares deeply about you but who isn't the soul mate of your dreams to find what's behind the curtain? If you don't find your dream mate behind the curtain, or it doesn't work out, you have nothing.

In real life, people thought then—and still believe—you could make the wrong decision. But on "Let's Make A Deal," there were no wrong decisions; no dire consequences.

Too many people simply don't realize that real life is no different than that game show—there are *no wrong decisions*! Before 1992, I was too paralyzed to actually leave a lucrative law practice that was making me miserable, to try something else. What if I made the wrong decision? How would I support my family? How could I start again? Then, I suffered through a year of surgeries, chemotherapy, radiation and disability. The lucrative law practice all but disappeared as, one-by-one, clients found that they couldn't wait indefinitely for my health to improve.

Would it have been any worse if I had chosen a different career? No. Who knows, I might have joined a company that provided a generous disability package and allowed me to work part-time as I recovered. In that case, staying in the law practice would have been interpreted as having been the wrong decision. Was it what was in the box or what was behind the curtain? It doesn't matter. What matters is choosing the one you *feel* will be the right one—saying "yes" to your dreams.

And what happens if your decision leads you to a place that's no better—or maybe worse—than where you were before you started pursuing your dream. Are you stuck? Permanently committed? NO!

You get to choose <u>again</u>—this time between what's behind the curtain and what's behind one of the stage doors. And whichever you choose, if you do it from your heart, you will have made the right choice.

Many years ago, one of my clients, Paul, was the manager of a trucking company owned by his father-in-law. The company was in serious financial trouble, but Paul had an offer from a competitor that was willing to pay him much more money to do the same work.

Paul had studied to be a chef. He was a large man who adored good food and was passionate about its preparation. He had worked in a few restaurants but had not been happy having his creativity hampered by a restaurant owner or manager. He dreamed of someday owning his own restaurant. *But* there were bills to pay and a family to support, so he committed himself, tentatively, to work for the new trucking company.

Then, one day while he was having a cup of coffee at a local diner, Paul learned that the owner wanted to sell the diner. The more questions he asked, the more he was sure he could scrape together the down payment and have his dream. He pictured himself catering local parties to rave reviews, baking pies that were the talk of the town, and packing his little diner to taste the unusual fare he had in mind for it.

The fear factor was strong, but the pain of doing the same work—work he never loved—for the rest of his life was too great, so Paul bought the diner.

The venture failed. Paul simply couldn't sell enough cups of coffee to pay the monthly costs and had to close his doors. Now, there was no trucking company job and no diner. Soon, however, there were offers from restaurants willing to give Paul some freedom over the menu and allow him to use his creativity.

A few years later, Paul and a partner started a successful wholesale restaurant supply business on the side. There were no wrong decisions.

4. _Fear of being rejected—an outcast, alone_. The woman at work to whom you are so attracted might say "yes" if you simply approach her and ask her out. But you're too afraid she won't—so you don't call.

The "big sale" might be right there in the "cold call" you need to make, but you're afraid they might hang up on you—so you hang up even before you connect.

The break you've been waiting for your entire career might be in that next audition or interview, but you're afraid they'll turn you down flat—so you don't show up.

If you take that promotion, your buddies at work will be afraid to talk to you. You'll be an outcast. So, you let it pass.

If you end the nowhere relationship to which you've been clinging for years to start again, you'll be—alone. And you're so afraid of being alone, you stay, unfulfilled and unhappy, in your safe neighborhood.

But if you don't do these things, you'll surely suffer the pain of never having at least tried them. And if you do what I'm hoping you'll do—get past your fear and pursue your dreams aggressively, I have no doubt that you will succeed.

My younger daughter Madeline, a teenager, is another actor. Each week she goes on at least one and sometimes as many as four auditions. While she has appeared on some popular television dramas and in one small movie, the number of times she hears "yes" is extremely small compared to the number of times she hears "Thank you" (That's what they say instead of "no"). Yet, each week, she goes on those auditions.

Madi knows that there must be several negative responses before she gets to a "yes." In a way, she knows that each "no" is bringing her closer to the "yes" that must inevitably come; and although that doesn't make it less painful or frustrating, she continues to tolerate the rejection because she knows the eventual acceptance will allow her to live her dream.

Let yourself suffer a rejection or two. Risk being alone. Risk being an outcast. All of these things can be fixed. Missing all of your chances to try to make your life better cannot be fixed.

5. _Fear that we don't deserve to be happier._ We grew up on stories about people who went "too far." Icarus flew too high. His wings melted and he fell to his death. How about the guy who is warned to be nice to the people he meets on the way up because they are the same people he will see on the way back down again? We come to believe—to fear—that if we go further than we were "meant to go," we'll suffer in some way; we'll be struck down.

Added to the fear we've derived from "lessons" about flying too high, is the baggage we carry with us from childhood in the form of negative self-images.

Michael, another good friend of mine, has been married to the same woman, his second wife, Lillian for 15 years. Except for very superficial things—having dinner together and sharing the occasional movie—Lillian has made it clear that she is not interested in having any kind of relationship with him. Michael is unhappy. He asked Lillian to go for counseling with him, but her response was, *"I don't need counseling. I know what I want. You need counseling."*

One day, we were sitting outside at the same Chinese restaurant where my friend David challenged me to take the high dive. I was listening to Michael complain, as I had many times before. I asked him why he stays with Lillian if he's so unhappy and dreams of having a deep, caring relationship. He is not a young man, but he is still young enough to find someone who wants to make him happy. He is a caring, sensitive person with a great sense of humor.

While he was making excuses in response to my question, a thought struck me. I knew that Michael grew up with a severe speech impediment. A few years ago he underwent a medical procedure and therapy that changed his life by making the problem of a whole lifetime all but impossible to detect. He has become a good salesman and boldly makes sales presentations the very thought of which once would have frightened him into hiding. Maybe, I thought, he believes that he deserves to suffer in his relationship with Lillian. After all, Lillian married him when he could hardly talk. So I asked him, *"Michael, are you making all of these excuses because maybe—deep down inside—you're afraid you don't deserve to be happier?"*

Tears welled up in Michael's eyes. It was true! He was afraid to end this relationship—to find something better—because he was afraid he didn't deserve anything better!

It's the same everywhere. I was the last to be chosen for a team in every sport. I was overweight, slow and uncoordinated. As a child, especially as a male, the inability to play ball leaves you with incredibly poor self-esteem. You grow up believing that the athletic kids—the ones with sports skills and muscles—are the ones who deserve to be happy, not you. And you can actually be afraid that if you pursue your dream, you'll be asking for more happiness than you deserve!

Erica, another friend, was not attractive by high school standards. She was never asked to the Prom and was painfully lonely. Now in her 30s and "unattached," she recently started dating a man who has everything she ever dreamed she'd find in the man with whom she'd want to spend her life. He's Cinderella's handsome Prince, with humor and charm. Erica began, however, to pretend to be unavailable, making lame excuses when he called her for a date. Clearly, this was not a case of keeping the flame alive by playing hard to get. Erica was sabotaging the relationship.

I asked her directly why she was destroying what seemed to be a perfect relationship and she replied honestly, as she believed, *"I'm putting an end to it before I get really hurt. This is never going to go anywhere."*

So, you dream of being with your handsome prince or of having that CEO spot, but you don't pursue your dream because you're afraid that *you might not deserve it,* and that something "bad" will happen if you even think about it.

But how can it be that some people are entitled to happiness and some are not? Every one of us deserves to be as happy as we can be. We deserve to achieve our dreams and then to dream new ones we can pursue. If you are making excuses because you you're afraid that you are not entitled to be happier, recognize it for what it is, scold yourself for thinking and feeling that way, and then forgive yourself and start living your life.

6. *Fear that we're inadequate.* The "circumstance excuse" often grows out of this fear. ("…. BUT, I'm not good enough, not ready, not trained enough…").

Maybe it was foolish for Robert J. Zimmerman to be pursuing his dream of becoming a folk singer. He was a decent songwriter and an adequate guitarist, but when he tried to sing it was obvious to everyone that he had a great deal of difficulty staying on key, sustaining notes and doing those great things with his voice that folk singers did.

It made more sense for him to write songs for his friend, Joan Baez, and for folk groups like Peter, Paul and Mary. But he wanted to perform his own work. If he had feared that he wasn't good enough, few people would have come to know Bob Dylan.

Imagine if Thomas Edison had feared that his lack of a formal education made him unfit to be an inventor or if Colonel Sanders had thought that his age made it impossible for his chicken franchise idea to succeed.

Yet the fear that we're not *capable* of living our dream plagues all too many of us.

7. *Fear of success.* Yes! A great number of people who are not living their dreams are more afraid of success than they are of failure. Many of the people who say they fear that they might fail are actually more afraid of succeeding.

Think about this: if you're conditioned to back away from the things you are afraid of, being afraid of *failure* would cause you to back as far away from failure as you could. You'd be <u>very</u> successful.

What about succeeding could possibly make someone afraid of it? You're getting what you dreamed of. How could you be afraid of that?

The fear of success is usually related to other fears. You just might achieve your dream. If you have that money you wanted to make your life more comfortable, will you still have your friends? (*Fear of rejection, fear of being alone and different, or fear of change*). If you make it to that Vice President position, will you be able to hold onto it? Can you stand the pressure? (*Fear of failing in the future and fear of being embarrassed*).

Some of us are so afraid of success that we sabotage our efforts when we're almost there. We snatch impossible passes out of the air, carrying the ball all the way down the field and then drop the perfect pass as we cross the goal line.

As a lawyer, I finally landed that high profile case, against one of the largest and most influential firms in the state. It was the case that could bring my career to a whole new level. My clients, two partners in a very large, successful accounting firm, were satisfied that I was the right attorney for them. They were not worried that their ex-partner had hired the "Big Guns." They even laughed about how much he was paying per hour to have a 50-year old attorney carry the briefcase of the 60-year old attorney to the courtroom. I, however, spent an inordinate amount of time and effort trying to convince my clients *not to worry* about the big law firm on the other side. They hadn't been worrying, but began to, because *I* was making such a big deal about it. Eventually, they transferred their case to a large law firm that had the same perceived "clout" as their ex-partner's lawyers.

I could have complained about another piece of bad luck, but even back then I understood that *I* had *created* that bad luck, because I was afraid of succeeding.

There are, of course, many reasons for self-sabotage that do not have to do directly with fear of success. These include guilt about doing better than someone else in your family; a family history of failure that creates a pattern you feel compelled to follow; a need to "defy" your parents, to name a few. Fear of success, then, can be in good company.

Another aspect of the fear of success is the fear of the emptiness on the other end once we get what we want. At the movies as a small boy—a large, small boy—I would buy a bar of chocolate molded with little bite-size squares in it. I would eat the bar very slowly; a square during the previews, a square at the beginning of the movie, a square after the first victim was eaten by the monster…and so on. I was afraid that once the whole bar was gone, I'd be disappointed.

Some of us do the same thing with our dreams. We never quite reach them because we're afraid that once we do, we'll be disappointed.

There's no doubt that fear of success is often what we fear when we are making excuses instead of taking action.

Try this exercise now in the space provided for it in your *Dream Journal*:

EXERCISE 4. Look at each of your dreams and identify and write down which of the Paralyzing Fears you think might be holding you back from living it. What face is the fear that holds you back wearing?
Is it fear of:

Failing?

Being embarrassed?

Committing to the wrong thing?

Being rejected, alone or an outcast?

Not being worthy—that you don't <u>deserve</u> to succeed?

Success?

Or is it another fear? Write down all of the fears that might be holding you back for each dream.

> The secret of life isn't what happens to you,
> but what you do with what happens to you.
> ~Norman Vincent Peale~

Step Six: Identify the "payoffs" of your inaction.

Let's see what we know so far:

- We all have dreams.
- Some of them are hidden from us, but we have ways to draw them out.
- We are not pursuing many of these dreams because they are beyond our "safe neighborhood."
- Moving beyond our safe neighborhood always results in fear responses—the "fear factor."
- We've been conditioned to respond to the fear factor by taking its presence as a sign that something is not okay, and by "backing away."
- This response is a <u>learned</u> response.
- We need to learn a new response when it comes to pursuing our dreams.
- The right response is to recognize that *it's okay to be afraid.* But if we're pursuing a dream, we *just have to do it*, despite the fear.

We also know what fears hold most people back, and we've explored the ones that are holding us back.

"I'm very smart now," you want to say, *"but nothing's changed. I have more insight, but I'm still paralyzed."*

Maybe part of the reason is that there's a <u>payoff</u> to letting your fears hold you back.

My friend, Fran, a woman in her 50s, has been overweight most of her adult life since giving birth to her daughter, Holly, who is now a teenager. Until very recently, she expressed unhappiness about her condition to everyone close to her. Her clothes from 20 years ago still hang in her closet, waiting for the time she can once again fit into them.

Fran would often project her concerns about weight onto her daughter Holly, scolding her for having too much dessert, or a second helping of pasta at dinner, despite the fact that Holly is not the least bit overweight. She's even a little on the thin side. As a result, of her mother's obsession, however, Holly is now obsessed about her appearance.

Fran had tried every diet and every exercise fad to lose weight. Usually, she'd stick to a diet or exercise program long enough to lose a few pounds and then abandon it—sometimes with a reason and sometimes without.

Most of the time, however, she'd starve herself all day and then treat herself to a massive dinner and a large bowl of ice cream as a nighttime snack. Then, in the morning, she'd get on the scale and tears would roll down her cheeks. This would start another day of starving.

Fran had reached the point that it seemed as if she didn't care who she told about her unhappiness with her appearance. One day, I was able to take her aside to talk about it. It seemed that she was afraid to pursue her dream of being in shape. But why?

"I know you dream of fitting into the old clothes you have in your closet, Fran," I started, *"But you seem to be afraid to do what you need to do to make your dream come true."*

"Afraid? I'm not afraid to lose weight," she protested, *"I just can't do it. I've tried everything over the years and nothing works."*

I asked Fran if a doctor had ever told her she had a thyroid or other problem preventing her from reaching her goal. *"No,"* she replied, and then added, a little miffed, *"but he told me that this was just my natural size based on how my mother and grandmother were."*

Then, I asked her about her diets and exercise programs. She confided that they were boring and left her hungry (the diets) or sore (the exercise programs) or both. It was just too painful to stick to them—especially since the likelihood was she'd either have to stay on a program like that for the rest of her life or would gain any weight she lost right back.

I pointed out to Fran that she had just expressed several fears: the fear of continued pain of deprivation; the fear of failing; the fear of committing to something that she may not be able to continue. I could have talked to her about underlying fears. The fear of being successful in her efforts, and how it might change her life and her relationship with her husband, Neil—and maybe her relationship with her daughter, but something else was bothering me, so I held back and let her talk some more.

"I just want to walk on the beach this summer without feeling that I look like a beached whale," Fran blurted out, *"That's what would make me happy."*

I continued to have the feeling that even if Fran did <u>Exercise 3</u> and compared the pain she was suffering by not pursuing her dream with the pain she would suffer sticking to a diet and exercise program, she would still opt to claim that no program would work. There was something more here I wasn't sure I was getting.

Then, it struck me. There was a "payoff" to <u>not</u> achieving her dream. Fran was the hopeless, hapless "victim" of genes and metabolism, and she'll yell and scream her denials when she sees this section of the book, but she <u>loved</u> the *attention* she got in that role. Fran was getting *everyone's* attention by not being able to have her dream. We consoled her, and offered her our advice and felt sorry for her. She was getting what she wanted even more than her dream of fitting into those old clothes in her closet. And she would never pursue her dream, because her *biggest* fear was that she wouldn't get attention anymore if she ever achieved her dream.

I thought immediately of another friend, Larry, a lawyer who was complaining about how much he hated practicing long before I made <u>my</u> decision to change careers.

Larry is a sole practitioner who doesn't necessarily want to stop practicing, he just wants to work in a firm where he doesn't have to look for business—where the work is fed to him and his income is relatively steady and assured.

Larry and I (and his other friends) have spent many a lunch in conversations that go something like this:

Larry: *I'm so sick of practicing alone. It's lonely. If I could just get into a firm where I'd have steady business and people to talk to.*

Sandy:	*Have you looked around at all, Larry?*
Larry:	*There's nothing out there for someone who's been at it as long as I have.*
Sandy:	*Where have you tried?*
Larry:	*Oh, I've tried, believe me. Not recently, but what's the point? Why*
	would it be any better now than it was a few years ago? If anything, it would be worse.
Sandy:	*Well, how would you know unless you tried?*
Larry:	*I suppose you're right. Maybe I will look again. The biggest problem is not getting enough business.*
Sandy:	*Larry, do you say things like this to your clients when you're with them?*
Larry:	*What clients? (Pretending to laugh) Sure, I say it. It's the truth, isn't it?*
Sandy:	*Can I suggest to you that it would be better if you made them feel you were successful?*
Larry:	*I guess that's true. I just wish I knew what I could do about it.*
Sandy:	*Have you tried asking the clients you've helped to suggest referrals?*
Larry:	*That never works. I just don't have the kind of clients who know people who can afford my services.*
Sandy:	*What about advertising?*
Larry:	*That's another expense and unless you're in a negligence-type practice, you never get any business from it.*
Sandy:	*Have you tried it?*

Larry: No, not really....

Larry and Fran are in similar situations. Their dreams are clearly defined and both are extremely afraid. But their ability to say, *"This is my dream, I have to pursue it,"* is hampered by their perception of the payoff they receive from being victims of circumstances that keep them from reaching their dreams. They are being rewarded for making excuses. The reward—the attention they receive from friends and family—is so seductive, they are afraid they'll lose it if they achieve their dreams. Clearly, in their perception, the pleasure of staying where they are outweighs the anticipated pain of pursuing their dreams.

But I've used the word "perception" in connection with the payoff because I believe that neither Larry nor Fran is seeing his or her situation clearly. Larry had extensive abdominal surgery several years ago to save his life. He was suffering from abdominal problems the cause for which was never clearly established. Now, he is being considered as a candidate for dialysis and kidney transplantation. His kidneys are failing and there is no clear medical explanation for this condition.

Of course, these health problems can occur in individuals who have always pursued their dreams, but the years of unhappiness could not possibly have helped Larry's immune system.

Fran's situation is, thankfully, not as severe, but her unhappiness—arising mostly from not pursuing her dream—pervades her household, straining her relationship with Neil and Holly. I'm certain that it has not helped her relationships with other family members or friends, either.

All of us need to decide whether the payoffs for not pursuing our dreams—particularly the attention we get from being victims of our circumstances--are more important to us than the dreams themselves. If we prefer the payoffs, we'll never live the dream, but at least we'll be honest about it. The next exercise addresses this question.

EXERCISE 5. Reexamine the dreams you have been building in your Dream Journal, and find the section for each dream marked "Payoffs I am receiving by not pursuing my dreams." List all of the small pleasures you may be receiving for not pursuing your dreams. Here are a few ideas:

"I get lots of attention and sympathy from friends and family."
"I overeat (drink, etc.) as a consolation for the misery caused by my inability to take action on my dreams."
"I don't have to face my fears"
Now, decide: Are you willing to give up these payoffs. If you are, say so in writing on the bottom line of the "Payoff" section.

> He has not learned the lesson of life
> who does not every day surmount a fear.
> ~Julius Caesar~

Step Seven: Identify the Hardships, Roadblocks, Obstacles and Other Excuses in your life.

The BIG Roadblock: The people we love

My little five-year old heart was pounding, because my mother had just told me we were going to Coney Island. That meant amusement parks and rides, and the chance to get on my favorite ride—the carousel.

Okay, so I wasn't a very adventurous five-year old! But this was no ordinary carousel. Nothing like the little sissy prefabricated plastic carousels of today. It was huge. To my little five-year old eyes, it was the size of…Yankee Stadium. It was constructed almost entirely out of wood and brass. The floor was hardwood, the horses were hand-carved and beautifully painted and at its center it had carved wooden panels that were painted in reds, blues and gold. There were colored neon and florescent lights in all the wooden beams holding up the wood canopy. The horses bobbed up and down on thick, shiny brass rails as the carousel swept around to the sound of a real old-fashioned calliope (that's a kind of musical device) playing circus music.

I could wear my little cowboy scarf and the hat with the chin strap—a string on each side connected with a wooden bead—pulled right up under my chin, and gallop through the night on my trusty steed, "Pinky." (No, I didn't <u>always</u> pick a pink horse. Sometimes it was "Greeny" or "Old Blue.")

I was excited, too, because I was finally big enough to ride on one of those big wooden horses all by myself—without my Mommy standing next to me. I could pick a horse in the middle row, right near where the big kids rode. Big kids picked the outside row, so that they could do one of the coolest things in the world: as the horses came around, they could reach up to a wooden arm that hung from the ceiling, just outside the carousel. Fist-sized metal rings were loaded into the wooden arm and dispensed from the end of it. As you rode around towards the point where the wooden arm hung in the air, you'd stand up on the metal stirrups, reach up to the dispensing end and pull down a ring.

Most of the time you'd get a black ring. But every once in awhile (actually every tenth time, but I thought it was just magic), you'd reach up and grab a ring that was *solid gold*! Well, I <u>believed</u> it was solid gold. I was only five.

It was a brass ring, the only real purpose of which was to get you a free ride. But to me, it was a magical symbol. By the time I was big enough to sit on one of the outside horses, the carousel was gone. For the rest of my life, though, the picture in my mind of kids on the carousel reaching for the brass ring reminded me that life could be filled with adventure, passion, joy and fulfillment—things I knew I wanted, even before I knew what they were.

As we grow, however, we make choices, most of which are based on how we deal with the tension between our dreams and our fears. I longed for the high diving board, but found my 8-foot diving board—as a lawyer handling 8-foot cases—and grew to hate my life. Time and again, the pull of my fears caused me to pass up my chances to grab for those rings; my opportunity to bring adventure into my life; to pursue something about which I was passionate; and to find joy and fulfillment.

One of my brass rings as an adult was a career where I would have all of those things—adventure, passion, joy and fulfillment—but I was too paralyzed to just reach up beyond the safe neighborhood of my personal carousel and grab for that ring! It's no surprise that my health gave out. I looked down the road on which I was traveling—and all I saw ahead of me were sixty-hour weeks of adventure-less, passionless, joyless, unfulfilling work, followed by death. My body just had to be saying, *"Why go on? Let's just end it now."*

I understand now that my inability to act on my dreams came from the way I responded to my fears. If I was afraid, *things were not okay* and, I believed, that I was _supposed_ *to back away* from the thoughts that were causing me to feel fear—*making excuses instead of taking action.*

But it's also true that the well-meaning people around me reinforced my response to my fears every day—making it ever more difficult to find a new way of responding to them. If I mentioned how unhappy I was, and my need to change my career, I would get responses that sounded something like these:

"Sandy, you've been a lawyer for years, you have hundreds of clients. You'd give all of that up to start something totally new—from the beginning?"

"Sandy, you're a lawyer. You don't know how to do any honest work! Who's going to hire you?"

"Sandy, it may be okay for you to go off and risk your own financial well being, but what about your children? Are you willing to risk their well being?

I finally closed my ears to those voices and reached for that ring, grabbing onto my chance for adventure, passion, joy and fulfillment. I found them all. When I did, it was for two reasons: first, because I was in too much pain not to; and then, because I came to understand that the <u>right</u> response to fear of pursuing your dreams is to *acknowledge that it's okay to be afraid, but if it's your dream you just have to do it, despite the fear.*

I also realized something about all those well-meaning friends and family members who had been discouraging me. All were really saying, *"<u>We</u> are afraid... for you and for ourselves. This is way outside your safe neighborhood and way outside ours, in which you play a big role. That's not okay. Back away."*

My own "mother" voice had been working on me, too. You know the one I mean, the one that says: *"Be careful, you're near a dark alley. You're crossing the street, look both ways. Never leave the house without clean underwear...."* When it came to my dream of changing careers, the voice was saying: *"Why do you have to do this? Why do you have to be happy; why can't you just settle on being 'content' like everybody else?"*

Is it any wonder I was paralyzed?

While we're working on exercises to get around that voice in our own heads—the fear factor voice—we need to also discuss a strategy for dealing with those people we care about whose view of us the way we are now is an integral part of <u>their</u> safe neighborhoods. These are people who may never have pursued their dreams. How will they understand our pursuit of ours?

A woman dreams of losing weight and begins to live her dream. Her husband thinks: *"She'll be beautiful and won't want me anymore."* The wife of the physician turned golf professional worries that her lifestyle will change and that she'll no longer be a "doctor's wife." The friends of a would-be entrepreneur worry that she'll no longer have time for them. Many of the issues your friends and family face are similar to the codependency issues families of recovering alcoholics and addicts face. Relationships have been built on who you are now—relationships that will need to change.

Here's another truth I've learned: where there is love, these relationships will last, and where there isn't, they won't. These people in your lives will not be comfortable. Not until you're actually succeeding in your quest and, maybe, even after you do. Don't let them stop you. They are calling to you to stop and back away— because their own fear factors are entwined with yours. You're moving beyond *their* safe neighborhoods. But the ones who really love you will be proud of your success—proud even if you try and don't succeed. You <u>will</u> succeed, though—you'll have anything you want if you try hard enough. Let go and believe in yourself.

Comfort the frightened people in your life and reassure them that the pursuit of your dream won't change the way you feel about them or the way you relate to them. A great way to get them to stop being afraid, and to stop saying things that "pull you back" is to put them to work helping you. Find something you need that they can help you with. Ask them to be "cheerleaders"—to encourage you and cheer you on. You'll be helping them as they help you. You might even inspire them to read this book and pursue their dreams. Whatever you do, *don't let them hold you back.*

More Roadblocks and Other Excuses.

The world is filled with opportunities. As my friend Marv points out, though, to many people, any of these can become "Stop-portunities." You can view the hardships, obstacles and roadblocks in your life as challenges or you can use them as your excuses. Among the roadblocks we put in our own path are these:

"It's not the right time…"

You've acknowledged the payoffs that keep you from your dreams and you've decided to push on past them and work on the people you love. But maybe this just isn't the right time. Maybe when you've become a little more comfortable. Maybe when you have a little more experience. Maybe it will be when the boss is in a better mood. Maybe when you have a little more money in the bank. Maybe when the moon is colonized. One of those things will make it the right time.

"Maybe when…" is your fear talking. The right time to start is TODAY. You may need to gather some things together for your journey beyond the borders of your safe neighborhood. Start today.

"But it <u>isn't</u> the right time," I hear you say. *"My daughter has just started college and I can't risk not having that income…"*
"My marriage is on shaky ground and this will end it…"
"I'm having health problems and I can't take any risks…"
"I'm taking care of my sick father and there's no time…"
"What I want takes money and I have none…"

Your fear continues to speak, giving you terrific excuses to make when there's action to be taken. Yes, it will be more difficult if these roadblocks are in your path. But <u>everyone</u> has roadblocks. What you do with them is what counts.

The "But" Monster

We've been talking about him on and off throughout this book, without actually mentioning his name, but I think it's time for you to finally meet the enemy—the "But" Monster. When you were little, your parent or some other adult posted a powerful monster at the border of your safe neighborhood. They cared for and fed him and then taught you how to do it. Over the years, you've given him an arsenal of weapons with instructions to keep you inside your Safe Neighborhood at all costs. He fires these powerful weapons—limiting words—at <u>you</u>, whenever you get too close to the border, and they come pouring out of your mouth with no thought whatsoever. *"But…,"* *"yes, but…,"* *"if only…,"* *"I'll try…"* and *"maybe when…"* are among his favorites.

"I'd really like to start interviewing," you say very honestly, since this is one of your dreams, "BUT*, unfortunately, I have way too much work to do this month."*

"YES, *I want to find a new job*, BUT *the economy is bad.*
MAYBE WHEN *it improves,* I'LL TRY *to do some looking around.*
IF ONLY *it were better.*"

The "But" Monster's favorite game is firing his weapons at you at times and in places and ways that you miss entirely. He just loves it when you don't notice he's doing his work and you <u>really believe</u> those words when they come out of your mouth.

BEWARE THE "BUT" MONSTER!

You've been caring for and feeding this monster all your life and he is virtually indestructible now. Your best defense against him is to spoil his game by recognizing when those limiting words are coming out of your mouth or floating around in your head. They are <u>his</u> words, not yours, and you can stop using them—or listening to them—if you choose. Start noticing when you use these limiting words and stop doing it!

Limiting Beliefs

While "but," "yes, but," "if only," "I'll try" and "maybe when" are limiting <u>words</u>, you are also being held back by limiting <u>beliefs</u>. Your fear causes you to give yourself powerful limiting messages.

"I stink at math," I hear one of my daughters' schoolmates say. Even if she has the potential to be a math genius, those words, expressing a "belief" that she can't do it, will stop her cold. It's possible that she really does not have the aptitude for math, but it is more likely that her "But" Monster has supplied her with a way to

deal with her fears—that her trouble with math is more likely a problem of fear than one of capacity.

Somewhere along the line it became too difficult to breeze through math. She had always been able to get "A"s with ease before and could still do it with most of her other classes, but it no longer worked with math, and she became discouraged. So she "turned off" to math. She was afraid, so she backed away. She's even more afraid now—either that she might find out that she really has a learning limitation, or that the extra effort she needs to make might be more work than she is willing to do. She may also be worrying that people will see how difficult math has become for her and think she's a "loser." It would be embarrassing. Then, there's the payoff for being able to say she stinks at something—lots of attention from friends who jump to assure her that she can do it if she tries.

Every time you hear yourself saying that you can't do something, one of two things is true: either you really can't do it, or you have some fear related to making yourself capable of doing it. But if you need to be able to do it to live your dream, you need to tell yourself that it's okay to be afraid—and then go do what you have to do.

EXERCISE 6. It's time to dig deeper into your fears. First, if you haven't been doing it already, tell the people in your life— the people you care about and who care about you—about your dreams and what you've been doing. Then, in the spaces provided for responses in your Dream Journal (starting on page 127), do the following for each dream listed:
(a) Identify the people in your life who express fear about your dreams in the things that they say, or in the way they respond

to you when you talk about your efforts to pursue them. These are the people you'll want to try to make your helpers and cheerleaders as you go along your path.

(b) What's stopping you from getting to work on your dreams immediately? Identify and list the hardships, roadblocks and obstacles in your life that are holding you back.

(c) What abilities, talents, skills, licenses, degrees that you think you need don't you have? Or, what do you believe you're just not good at that you need to be good at to live your dreams. Write them down in the space provided for you.

(d) What else do you believe is holding you back from living each of your dreams? Write these down, too.

Now, take a look at all of the things you've listed. Start with those fears expressed by the people you care about. Are any of them pursuing <u>their</u> dreams—or have they settled for the protection of their Safe Neighborhoods? How about those hardships, obstacles and roadblocks—Would they have stopped someone who had no fear? Has <u>anyone</u> you've ever heard of overcome similar obstacles to attain the same or similar dreams?

EXERCISE 7. Spend a week trying to catch yourself using limiting words, such as "but," "yes...but," "if only," "I'll try" and "maybe when." When you do, write them in the space provided in your Dream Journal on page 135. At the end of the week, review this page and spend the next few weeks making a conscious effort to find better words. Make yourself accountable. Stop using words that limit your potential.

> **D**o the thing you fear to do and keep on doing it...
> that is the quickest and surest way
> ever yet discovered to conquer fear.
>
> ~ Dale Carnegie ~

Step Eight: Take one step.

Congratulations again! If you've come this far in the book, you're ready to do what you need to do to change your life. It's time to get you started up the path to your High Diving Board. You'll need the key I was so fortunate to find—a key that will let you unlock the border gate to your Safe Neighborhood, charge past the "But" Monster, and get on your way to living your dreams.

What you have to do is actually pretty easy: Stop making excuses and

start taking ACTION!

"Well, duh!" you say, *"You've been saying that all along. If I could take action I wouldn't need you or this book."*

What you're really saying—asking—is *how* do I take action? What do I do *first*?

The answer is:

Do **ANYTHING!**

When I made my decision to pursue a career as a motivational speaker and writer, I was overwhelmed. How do you get past your old way of looking at fear when you're facing Mt. Everest and you don't know how to climb? Or, you're about to swim the English Channel, but you don't know how to swim?

The best first step is to take <u>any</u> action—in any direction. Start up the mountain. Jump into the water. Even if it's random, it gets you <u>moving</u>. You may not be headed in the right direction but you're not paralyzed—and that's a good thing.

For me, the first actions were to join Toastmasters and start attending meetings, and to buy books on how to become a seminar speaker and read them. It turns out that these were actions I needed to take anyway.

I wasn't certain whether the moves I was making were "right" or "wrong," but what counted for me—and what counts for you—was the movement. If you're moving, you're not paralyzed!

> Setting a goal is not the main thing. It is deciding how you will go about achieving it and staying with that plan.
>
> ~ Tom Landry ~

Step 9: Develop an Action Plan.

The secret to achieving your dreams is hidden in those tiny steps I took holding tightly to the rail of the wooden platform of my high diving board at The Quarry. My dream had become a goal—to take that dive! I had developed a simple plan: tell my daughter Stefanie I'm going to do it and bring her with me to witness it; walk up that path; and concentrate not on the ultimate outcome, but on each step. Stop thinking about getting all the way out on the board and think instead about taking <u>one</u> step. Then, think about taking the next. Step after tiny step. I was persistent; no matter how many times that infernal fear factor voice tried to stop me, I kept taking those steps. And suddenly, I was at the end of the board with nowhere to go but into the water.

I didn't realize it at the time, but I was following the classic success formula:

(1) Start by stating your dream as a clearly defined goal

(2) Develop a plan—even a very simple, naive plan—to reach the goal

(3) Take immediate action on that plan; and

(4) Persist until you reach the goal.

Earlier in this book, we talked about Thomas Edison's creation of the light bulb. Edison's dream was to create a viable source of light from electricity. He went about it according to the success formula:

(1) He stated his dream as a goal: *"I am going to find whatever it is that will allow me to use electricity as a source of light."* He wrote the goal in his laboratory notes. Then,

(2) He developed a simple plan to reach his goal: to test different materials and combinations of materials until he found one that gave him what he wanted.

(3) He took immediate action on his plan, by starting to test everything he thought might be a potential solution; and, perhaps most importantly,

(4) He persisted—continuing in the face of thousands of failed experiments—until he found a combination that worked. Edison was not the least bit surprised that he succeeded.

If the formula was good enough for Thomas Edison, I thought, it's good enough for me. I was already taking action—actually moving—but where to? How could I keep taking action when I had no clue how to get where I wanted to go and the borders of my safe neighborhood were always inches away? I needed a plan.

But how could I even create a plan, if I didn't see a clear path?

I started working *backward from my goal:* If I wanted to be a motivational speaker, I'd need to speak. If I wanted to speak, someone would either have to hire me to speak to his or her group or people would have to be willing to come see me. If I wanted them to be willing to come see me, they needed to know I was there and had something to offer. This meant having written materials, tapes, brochures, and a book. A BOOK? Hmmm... Now <u>there's</u> an idea!

I started to chart out what I thought I needed to do, changing it from time-to-time, as my understanding of what I needed to accomplish became clearer. Here's what it began to look like:

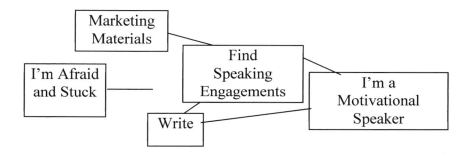

Then, I started working *forward*. I decided that I needed to speak and teach anywhere and to anyone about anything. I put in the steps I believed might get me to the ending I wanted, so that my plan started to look like this:

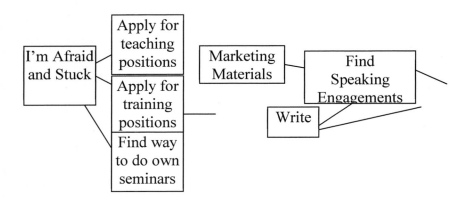

I developed several different resumes and scoured the newspapers for employment ads for college instructors, adult education instructors and corporate trainers, sending out resumes, going on interviews when I occasionally was granted one. I started my own speaking business, the Business Development Institute, and created motivational and informative programs.

Eventually, it developed into something like this:

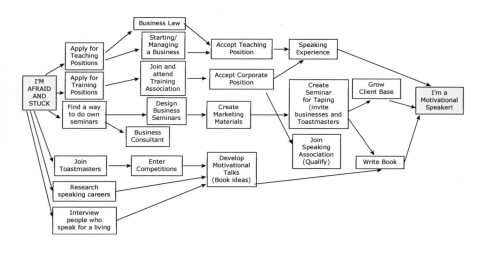

I hired myself out as a business consultant and studied coaching, at first to give me more opportunities to network for speaking engagements. I thought about a business book I loved that had influenced much of my new consulting business, *The E-Myth Revisited*, by Michael Gerber. I thought that I might love to teach its principles and help the author grow his consulting business, so I called Michael Gerber in California to make an appointment to see him, and flew across the country on borrowed money to meet with him. He asked me to do a presentation for him and I told him I'd do it right there, so he "buzzed in" his entire staff and gave me fifteen minutes to do a sample presentation. He hated it--and it hurt that he did, but... *I had the courage to borrow money and go to California to meet with him; I had the courage to say "yes" when he suggested I make the presentation; I had the courage to take action—instead of making excuses!*

If anyone had told me while I was standing outside the rehearsal room with Stefanie that I would be flying across the country to make a sales pitch for my speaking services to one of my favorite authors and his training team, I would have told them they were crazy. But there I was.

Where had all this courage come from? It just "happened" as my little action steps caused me to develop momentum. Each action step led me more easily to the next which, in turn, led even more easily to the next.

While "licking my wounds" from my West Coast reception, I received a phone call from home that NYU wanted me to teach a course for them. Look what was happening: I was taking action on my dream! My dream had become a goal. I was following a plan to gain exposure as a speaker so that I could move on towards my goal. I was taking massive action on my plan. And I was persisting.

I was teaching and now, I started booking speaking engagements through my business. I was also interviewing as a corporate trainer. And... I was <u>happy</u>! There was adventure in my life and I was doing things about which I was passionate. Not a bad formula, is it?

EXERCISE 8. Use the Action Plan pages (pages 136-141) in the Dream Journal at the end of this book to chart out simple plans for your dreams. Put your goal—the dream you <u>will</u> have soon—on the right. Start filling in the steps you know you need to take. When you hit one that seems insurmountable, think about some possible alternatives and put them in boxes above or below the one giving you trouble. Look at your plan every day. See where it needs to be expanded or changed and how much more detail you can add to it.

> Most of the important things in the world
> have been accomplished by people who have
> kept on trying when there seemed to be no hope at all.
>
> ~Dale Carnegie~

Step 10: Persist until your dream comes true.

Earlier in this book, I mentioned how Harland Sanders, known to most people by his honorary Kentucky title, "Colonel," started KFC when he was 65 years old. At the time his very few assets included the old chicken recipe he knew everyone loved, an old white car and an old, rumpled white suit. The Colonel knew he could sell his recipe, for a small, one-time fee, but he believed there was a better way to market it—sharing in the profit from the sale of chicken cooked his way with a willing restaurant owner. There was a <u>goal</u>.

Like Edison, Sanders had a simple <u>plan</u>: to travel from restaurant-to-restaurant throughout the South, offering to cook up his recipe for the owners until at least one owner made a percentage deal with him.

Even the Colonel's closest friends laughed at him:

"Colonel, you're too old to start a new business—especially one you don't know anything about."

"Colonel, you're an old man. Even if your silly idea worked, you'd never live long enough to see any real money from it."

"Colonel, nobody's going to <u>pay</u> you to use your recipe."

"Colonel, you don't know anything about the franchise business.

Heck, aside from how to cook it, you don't even know anything about chicken!"

But Sanders had his *goal* and his *plan*. All he needed was to take action and persist—and that he did. He traveled from city-to-city throughout the South, talking to restaurant owners, frying up chicken for them using his secret recipe. One hundred, two hundred, three hundred times... They all loved the chicken. Many offered to buy the recipe, but no one wanted to enter into a sharing arrangement with him based on sales using the recipe. Eight hundred... nine hundred... He'd wear his old white rumpled suit and sometimes sleep in the back of his beat up white car.

Imagine being turned down more than 900 times and getting up the next morning to try again. Would you call that persistence?

Finally, after more than a thousand demonstrations and samplings and "rejections," an owner agreed to try to sell the Colonel's chicken his way...and in a few years both were wealthy men.

Walt Disney knew that for a project the size of his theme park, he needed investors. After designing his park, and being laughed at by his banker, he took his drawings and plans and began to visit as many potential investors as he could until he had his money.

His goal: get the money to build his theme park.

His plan: visit and present his ideas to as many people as it took to raise the money.

His action: he started making presentations to anyone who would see him.

His persistence: it took more than 300 presentations.

His result: Well, you've probably visited a Disney park somewhere in the world. The company he built has gone on to produce movies, buy a television network and a Broadway theater complex, and produce several successful Broadway shows.

How about the Laney High School sophomore whose dream was to be a basketball star? His heart was broken when he was cut from the Varsity team, the Laney High School Buccaneers, and he vowed that he'd become the best basketball player anyone had ever seen.

To reach this goal, his plan was a simple one: practice the basics of the game until he'd mastered them. Every morning he got to school early, to practice before classes began. Then, he practiced again after school. In the summer, he convinced the coach to get him into the school early each morning, so he could practice before going to work at his summer job. He practiced the basics all summer long. In the Fall, as a Junior, he easily made the team, but he kept up his endless practicing of dribbling, foul shots and lay-ups. And when he played in his senior year, some people said he was, indeed, the best basketball player they had ever seen. His name is Michael Jordan.

If you have a dream, it can be yours, if you follow the formula and persist, no matter what hardships you face or what obstacles and roadblocks are in your path. And if you're taking action instead of making excuses, you'll get past the fear that held you back from the start.

> I'm not the smartest fellow in the world,
> but I can sure pick smart colleagues.
>
> ~Franklin Delano Roosevelt~

6. More tips for getting past your fears.

The power of positive messages

Part of your fear factor is the voice in your head, that incessant parental voice that keeps telling us what we can't do—a voice Susan Jeffers calls the "chatterbox." It's the voice that tells you what you're doing is dangerous and will hurt you, even though all you're doing is what you were always meant to do—pursuing your dreams. Notice when you hear the voice and talk back to it. Tell it you <u>can</u> live your dreams, that you <u>are</u> doing it. Remember that this is just one element of the fear factor and--it isn't real!

In the depth of my depression, caused by my inability to take action, I told a friend about the voice that was holding me back. "How do you know," she asked, "that the voice is right? Where did it get its information?"

She was right. <u>I</u> created my fear factor voice and <u>I</u> gave it all of its information. How could <u>it</u> know something I'm sure can't be right?

A cornerstone of neurolinguistic programming, which really does work for many people, is to *talk back to the voice;* to give it positive messages to counteract the negative. You can't get the voice to stop sending you negative messages. But if you keep bombarding it with positive ones, you'll override it in your subconscious mind. That's why you hear people talking about positive affirmations.

Fight the negative chatter with positive words. Think them, say them out loud, write them down and look at what you've written. This is not "new wave" nonsense. It's a scientifically proven, effective way to override that Fear Factor voice. Your voice is saying, *"Don't do this; it's a mistake. You're making the wrong decision. You'll be sorry!"* Respond by saying things like this:

> *"This is my dream. I must do it, even if I'm afraid."*
> *"I am doing it and succeeding."*
> *"I am getting stronger and better every day."*
> *"I deserve this, and I will have it."*
> *"There are no wrong decisions."*
> *"I can handle anything that happens"*

Your subconscious will believe what it hears, so feed it lots of positive support in the present tense. It's harder to be afraid when your subconscious is convinced that you're on the right path and can't fail.

Make it about someone else.

Whatever your dream is, there is likely to be an aspect of it that involves other people. Your dream of finding the perfect partner is probably one of finding someone you can make happy. Your dream of finding the perfect job is one of being really useful to some organization somewhere. Even your dreams to quit smoking or to lose weight have elements of being able to please someone else while you're pleasing yourself.

Focus on the part that has to do with others and start doing for them. Volunteer. Give—your time, your love, your support, your acceptance, your forgiveness, and your attention. Be patient with people.

If you're focusing on others while you're pursuing your dream, you may suddenly find that you are on the way—and didn't even know it.

On September 11, 2001, firemen rushed into the World Trade Center Towers to save whatever lives they could. Afraid or not, their focus was on the victims. They did not allow themselves time to think about the dangers.

How much easier it is for those of us who are facing fears that don't (hopefully) include death. It's okay to be afraid, but focusing on others will pull you into action.

Surround yourself with positive people.

In Chapter 5, we talked about the people holding you back, and I suggested that you try to make them your "cheerleaders." We were discussing the people in your life with whom you have close relationships. The people who you know care about you, and the ones who are special to you.

When it comes to pursuing your dreams, the rest of the world is filled with three kinds of people:

- The ones who have no interest one way or another in your dreams—the great majority of people "living lives of quiet desperation," as Thoreau saw them;

- The ones who are negative influences—who will tell you your dream isn't possible, or is possible but too difficult to achieve—whether because they are afraid themselves or envious, just plain negative or malicious; and
- The ones who want to see you make your dreams come true—who even want to help you make your dreams come true, as I do.

You need to avoid the negative people and seek out those people filled with positive energy. Often, these are people who are, themselves, very successful, but whether they are or they aren't, surround yourself with them.

As a young law clerk, I became friends with a court secretary. My friend, Marie, was near retirement age and had lived through the Depression in the 1930s. Her years of want, so very long ago, compelled her to keep an entire grocery story of canned, frozen and boxed foods in her basement, which was set up with aisles, just like a supermarket.

Marie believed in me and assured me constantly that I could have whatever I wanted in life. She'd take me—and sometimes my wife, Hannah—"shopping" in her basement "store," insisting that we accept the free food to help us get wherever it was we dreamed of going. She never doubted we could—and would—have anything we wanted.

Find your Marie!

A few years ago, I found Toastmasters International. People join a Toastmasters club with *personal* goals—to learn to overcome their fear of public speaking and to be better at it, or to learn "leadership" skills. But something magical happens when they join. They start helping *other people* overcome their fears—and everyone begins to work together. Success becomes a team effort—an effort that comes to include other dreams, besides the public speaking dream.

The same thing happens in many church organizations and other groups. The key is to surround yourself with people who are positive and want to cheer you on and help you achieve your dreams.

Where can you go to find people like this? Why aren't you there yet? Get going!

Find a Mentor or Role Model

Find a mentor—someone who has achieved the dream you are dreaming. Better still, if you can't find one, *hire* one. The International Coaches Federation has a list of thousands of personal coaches who will help you get where you want to go. I make it a point to coach as many people as I can each year.

My father never asked anyone for help. I grew up believing that to be a man meant "toughing it out" myself. It wasn't until I decided to change careers that I <u>asked</u> anyone to help me. I was <u>afraid</u> to ask—afraid that I'd be imposing. When I did ask, I was amazed at what happened: people *wanted* to help me. It gave them pleasure to help. Not everyone and not always—but most of the people I asked, most of the time. If I succeeded, they would feel great that they had been a part of the success. Well, that's the way <u>I</u> was. Why did it surprise me that there were more people in the world like me?

Surrounded by cheerleaders, a team of people who are willing to help you succeed, and a coach-mentor or two, how can you fail? You can't. You won't.

Record and Reward

If you've been working in your Dream Journal, you've by now come to recognize the power of the written word as I have. Keep on recording your progress. On days when nothing has happened in the pursuit of your dreams, record that, too. On days when your efforts appear to have failed, record what happened. Remember that what we perceive as failures are learning experiences, so record what you learned from the experience.

Reward yourself when you've had success in one of your small steps. If you've lost another pound and something sweet would make you happy, have it. Hold off buying that new pair of shoes you wanted until you've completed a step you've been afraid to take. Then, use it as your reward.

Beware of Fear's first cousin, Guilt.

Next to fear, guilt is the biggest inhibitor of action. We feel guilty that we're not doing what our family wants us to do; we feel guilty that we're pulling away from—or ahead of—the people who are afraid for us.

There are thousands of reasons to feel guilty. As you grow and move on towards your dreams, relationships are bound to change, and you'll feel guilty: about having less time for the kids while you're taking classes; about working on your book at lunch instead of getting together with your "buds"; about starting that new business despite Mom's admonishment that it's a terrible idea; and about the fact that you may be taking a cut in pay at the "expense" of your family.

Guilt is one of the many roadblocks and obstacles you'll need to overcome—but don't let it be your excuse not to take action. When that feeling comes upon you, remind yourself again that you deserve to have your dream. It's much more selfish not to live the life you wanted to live, blaming the people who made you feel guilty, than it is to get what you want out of life so that you can be free to give what you want to the people you care about.

Trust in the principles expressed in this book.

In Chapter 5, I gave you my Ten Steps to Living Your Dream:

Step One:	Put it in writing.
Step Two:	Remember your dreams.
Step Three:	Explore the underlying dreams.
Step Four:	Feel your pain.
Step Five:	Identify what it is you're afraid of.
Step Six:	Identify the "payoffs" of your inaction.
Step Seven:	Identify the Hardships, Roadblocks, Obstacles and Other Excuses in your life.
Step Eight:	Take One Step.
Step Nine:	Develop an Action Plan
Step Ten:	Persist until your dream comes true.

The ten-step program in this book <u>works</u>—if you let it. I've used the basic principles to help many people overcome their fears. There's a scene in a movie I enjoy where there's a bridge across an endlessly deep chasm, but the bridge is invisible. The hero of the story steps off the edge on one side and appears to walk across the chasm in mid-air. To help his comrades, he sprinkles dust on the invisible bridge so that they can see that it's there.

Your invisible bridge is waiting for you. I hope I've sprinkled enough dust so that you can see that it's really there. You won't fall into the chasm. Come join me on the other side.

> The mass of men live lives of quiet desperation...
> and go to their graves without ever having sung their song.
>
> ~Henry David Thoreau~

7. Action Hero Birthday Party

It's your One Hundredth Birthday Party! You're in a large ballroom at a hotel not far from your home, surrounded by everyone you'd want with you on this very special occasion. Your children—grandparents themselves—are there with your grandchildren, who have brought their children. There are three generations of nieces and nephews and friends of all ages sitting at tables throughout the room. You are at the dais, at the front of the room.

One of your great grandchildren stands up and calls out to you, *"Grandma (or Grandpa) tell us the story of your life."*

You get some help to stand at the podium and begin your story. What will it be about? What will you say you did? What will you say you learned? Of what will you be proudest?

There can really be only two kinds of Hundredth Birthday Party stories—the story of an "Action Hero" or the story of one of life's victims—a "Victim of Fear."

Yours can be a story of pursuing your dreams: writing them down and using them as your compass to keep your life on course, taking some small action every day to reach them. There will surely have been times when you fell on your face, but you got back up again and kept taking action. You will have continued despite the many hardships life has in store for you, overcoming obstacles and finding your way around the many roadblocks in your path. But now, standing here at your Hundredth Birthday Party, you are able to speak with passion and a sense of accomplishment, telling the people you love that you've taken from life what you wanted and gave what you wanted, too! Yours is the story of an Action Hero.

You have joined the ranks of true Action Heroes, people who have overcome the obstacles and hardships in their paths to make better lives for themselves—people like:

Helen Keller, who despite becoming deaf and blind as an infant, grew up to become a world-renown author and speaker;

Colonel Sanders, destitute at age 65, but a millionaire in his seventies;

Anna Maria Robertson, a 78-year old widow in the 1930s, whose arthritis forced her to stop embroidering. She took up painting instead and became a respected artist in the 1930s, Grandma Moses. This, when she was in her eighties;

Winston Churchill, who overcame a childhood stutter to become one of the 20th Century's great orators and leaders; and his contemporary,

Franklin Delano Roosevelt, who was crippled by polio…after age 39 he could not get out of his chair…but he was, nevertheless, elected President of the United States four times.

These were true Action Heroes.

Hopefully, your hardships, obstacles and roadblocks were not as overwhelming as theirs, but your Hundredth Birthday Party story can still be one of a true Action Hero.

Or… you can look your grandchildren and great grandchildren in the eyes and tell the story of how you were afraid of falling on your face, so you played it safe. You'll use—as you always have—the hardships, obstacles and roadblocks in your life to make excuses for not taking—or haven taken—action. It will be a *"Woulda... Coulda... Shoulda... BUT..."* story. You'll talk about your long years, but without passion or joy. You won't say the words, *"I don't think my existence made much of a difference in this world...I didn't really live the life I wanted to live...I didn't get what I wanted and wasn't able to give what I wanted..."* but in every word you do utter, the Victim Story will be evident to anyone who listens closely. Your grandchildren and great grandchildren will hear clearly the unspoken admonition, *"I hope you have someone better to use as your role model."*

Could there be anything more painful than having to tell the Victim Story at your Hundredth Birthday Party?

"But," you may still be saying, *"how do you know what hardships you're going to face—illness, layoffs, depression...anything can keep you from fulfilling your dreams."*

Here's my final "High Diving Board" revelation:

You can write your Hundredth Birthday Party story today!

You know where you are now and you know where you want to be—what dreams you want to live. Write the story that you will tell when they call you to the podium on that special day.

Okay, I admit that some of the middle chapters will be missing. You won't know what hardships, obstacles and roadblocks you'll face along the way. But if it's a true Action Hero story, it won't matter, because you'll overcome the hardships, climb over the obstacles and find your way around the roadblocks to reach the same ending.

And your personal Hundredth Birthday Party Story will serve as your compass—the guide for every action you take throughout your life. You'll go off course and stop along the way, but you'll always get back on your path, because telling the Victim story would just be too painful.

For your last exercise, I'm asking you to write your personal Action Hero story; the story you want to be able to tell at your Hundredth Birthday Party:

EXERCISE 9. Write your Hundredth Birthday Party Story on page 143 in your Dream Journal. What dreams will have come true? What will you say you did during your life? What will you say you learned? Of what will you be most proud?

If your heart is set on the high diving board, don't settle for the low board or get stuck diving from the eight-foot board. Write down your dreams. Take action on them every day. Keep an action journal—a journal of your journey and your progress. When you fall, get up again and keep going. Put your Hundredth Birthday Party Story in your sights and get back to it. Do something—ANYTHING—towards making your life what you dream it will be.

I hope I'm there to wish you a Happy Birthday!

DREAM JOURNAL

DREAM JOURNAL

I have dreams I want to come true, but I have been afraid to take the action I know I need to take to make that happen.

I've made up my mind to read The High Diving Board, to do the exercises in this Dream Journal, and to start to pursue my dreams until they come true.

I will persist until it happens.

This is a commitment I am making to myself. I'm putting it in writing so that it's real to me.

I will succeed, because I've learned that it's okay to be afraid, but when it comes to my dreams, I have to do what I need to do anyway.

Date: _____ _____

(Your Name)

(See pages 35-37)

(See Preliminary Exercises on page 43)

When I was a child, I was passionate about

I am least happy today with

_____

_____

_____

_____

_____

_____

What I want most that I don't have already are

_____

_____

_____

_____

_____

_____

What I'd like my life to look like

~A year from now

_____

_____

_____

_____

_____

~in two years

_____

_____

_____

~in five years

_____

_____

_____

_____

~in ten years

_____

_____

_____

_____

~in twenty years

_____

_____

_____

How do I feel about

~my relationships

_____

_____

_____

_____

~my income

~my work

~my education

~my spiritual life

What would make them even better:

~my relationships

~my income

~my work

~my education

~my spiritual life

_____

_____

_____

Three Dreams I have been afraid to pursue:

1. _____

_____

2. _____

_____

3. _____

_____

(See Exercise 1 on page 46)

(For assistance on pages 126-134,
read pages 52-92 and complete Exercises 3-7)

Dream 1:

_____

_____

My dream redefined:

_____

_____

_____

The pleasure I'll have if I pursue my dream:

_____

_____

_____

The pain I'll suffer if I don't:

_____

_____

_____

Paralyzing fears that are holding me back from pursuing this dream:

_____

_____

_____

_____

Payoffs I'm receiving for not pursuing this dream:

_____

_____

_____

_____

The people in my life who are afraid - for me and for themselves:

_____

_____

_____

_____

The hardships, obstacles and roadblocks I tell myself are keeping me from going after this dream immediately:

_____

_____

_____

_____

The abilities, skills, licenses and degrees I tell myself I need before I can start:

_____

_____

_____

Other things holding me back from pursuing this dream:

_____

_____

_____

_____

Dream 2:

_____

_____

My dream redefined:

_____

_____

_____

The pleasure I'll have if I pursue my dream:

_____

_____

_____

_____

The pain I'll suffer if I don't:

_____

_____

_____

_____

Paralyzing fears that are holding me back from pursuing this dream:

_____

_____

_____

_____

Payoffs I'm receiving for not pursuing this dream:

_____

_____

_____

_____

The people in my life who are afraid - for me and for themselves:

_____

_____

_____

The hardships, obstacles and roadblocks I tell myself are keeping me from going after this dream immediately:

_____

_____

_____

_____

The abilities, skills, licenses and degrees I tell myself I need before I can start:

_____

_____

_____

Other things holding me back from pursuing this dream:

_____

_____

_____

_____

Dream 3:

_____

_____

My dream redefined:

_____

_____

_____

The pleasure I'll have if I pursue my dream:

_____

_____

_____

The pain I'll suffer if I don't:

_____

_____

_____

Paralyzing fears that are holding me back from pursuing this dream:

_____

_____

_____

_____

Payoffs I'm receiving for not pursuing this dream:

_____

_____

_____

_____

The people in my life who are afraid - for me and for themselves:

_____

_____

_____

_____

The hardships, obstacles and roadblocks I tell myself are keeping me from going after this dream immediately:

_____

_____

_____

_____

The abilities, skills, licenses and degrees I tell myself I need before I can start:

_____

_____

_____

Other things holding me back from pursuing this dream:

_____

_____

_____

A week of avoiding limiting words:
Week of _____

(Note your use of limiting words like "but," "yes but," "I'll try," "if only" and maybe when"—when and how did you use them this week)

Day 1

_____

_____

Day 2

_____

_____

Day 3

_____

_____

Day 4

_____

_____

Day 5

_____

_____

Day 6

_____

_____

Day 7

_____

_____

(See Exercise 7 on page 92)

Dream 1: Action Plan

[Review pages 95-100. Follow the instructions in Exercise 8 on page 100 and begin at both ends of the chart on these two pages to fill in the steps between where you are now and your dream. Come back to this chart regularly to continue to fill in the details or transfer it to a larger sheet.]

I'm stuck here…

My Dream…

Dream 2: Action Plan

[Review pages 95-100. Follow the instructions in Exercise 8 on page 100 and begin at both ends of the chart on these two pages to fill in the steps between where you are now and your dream. Come back to this chart regularly to continue to fill in the details or transfer it to a larger sheet.]

I'm stuck
here…

My Dream…

Dream 3: Action Plan

[Review pages 95-100. Follow the instructions in Exercise 8 on page 100 and begin at both ends of the chart on these two pages to fill in the steps between where you are now and your dream. Come back to this chart regularly to continue to fill in the details or transfer it to a larger sheet.]

I'm stuck
here...

My Dream…

NOTES:

My Hundredth Birthday Party Story